LONDONOPOLIS

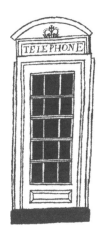

LONDONOPOLIS

A Curious History of London

MARTIN LATHAM

BATSFORD

TO MY WIFE

First published in the United Kingdom in 2014.
This paperback edition first published in the United Kingdom by
Batsford
43 Great Ormond Street
London WC1N 3HZ
An imprint of Pavilion Books Company Limited

ISBN 9781849944564

A CIP catalogue record for this book is available from the British Library

10 9 8 7 6 5 4 3 2 1

Reproduction by Mission Productions Ltd, Hong Kong
Printed and bound by 1010 Printing International Ltd, China

This book can be ordered direct from the publisher at the
website: www.pavilionbooks.com, or try your local bookshop.

Distributed in the United States and Canada by Sterling Publishing Co.,
1166 Avenue of the Americas, 17th floor, New York, NY 10036, USA

CONTENTS

ANCIENT LONDON

MEDIEVAL LONDON

TUDOR LONDON

ENLIGHTENMENT LONDON

VICTORIAN LONDON

TWENTIETH-CENTURY LONDON

THE SECRET THAMES

ACKNOWLEDGEMENTS

✦ ✦ ✦

I am ever-grateful to my PhD supervisor, Peter Marshall of Kings College London for teaching me to research. He and I often stayed in the old British Museum Reading Room until 9 pm, then walked out past Ramses' statue in the gloom. My father, a cockney bibliophile, numismatist and dowser, was a sergeant-major and sometime gravedigger who understood the city from the clay upwards. He also deserves space here.

In any endeavour, I remember my mother's perennial injunction: 'Don't worry if you don't fit into their sausage machine'. My brothers helped: John is a polymath who rediscovered an orchid on a roundabout, and taught me obscure poets and painters, Paul is a polemical conservation architect who has inspired me much and Mike, although Patton-esque, first told me about fairies in Holland Park when I was five. With Sarah, my sister, I have accomplished many enjoyable odysseys across the city.

Waterstones people have taught me about so many books and ideas: the company is my third university. I thank Tim Waterstone, the Sun King, for hiring me 26 years ago, and James Daunt for keeping it all going, like Cardinal Richelieu. Waterstones has led to conversations with David Mitchell,

Will Self, Jenny Uglow and Peter Ackroyd. They have all deepened my understanding of London. Ackroyd has moved London writing into a new-found land of poetic erudition. The old atrophy without the young: Josh Houston at Yale University Press has repeatedly broadened my horizons. The irrepressible Paul Maycock of Craenen is a fellow cartophile. Orc-like, I have mined Robert Sherston-Baker's labyrinthine Chaucer Bookshop and found unimagined treasures there. Suzi, Luke and Sarah run the best bookshop café in the world; much of the joy in this book comes from them.

I wrote this book whilst working full-time: Simon and Rachael Halle-Smith gave encouragement, potations and endless kindness. Jenny and Blaise carried on helping me even when their home flooded. Mark and Lorna Swain's house has been an oasis for the imagination. I thank my children: Ailsa and her Rivendellian husband Adam gave me confidence, the thought of Oliver's quick wit kept the book clear, India's enthusiasm is rooted in a dharma-level wisdom, Caspar's Chestertonian conversation inspired me, and William's humour kept melancholy at bay. My stepchildren endured my anecdotes, Francesca told me to write them down – possibly to shut me up – Jack brought me a wonderful artichoke dish and Sam makes great coffee.

Kate Gunning found out where you can see the Fleet River, and her friendship underpins the whole book. My agent Sophie Lambert is an eagle-eyed Yoda. At Batsford, Kristy Richardson was warmly supportive; Polly and Tina are my fairy godmothers. Joe McLaren added magic, humour and a poetic warmth to my text. My wife Claire gave love and understanding, and weeded the text of obscurities. In working full-time and running the house while I wrote she showed the endurance powers of two of her heroes, Dervla Murphy the traveller, and Kevin Costner in *Waterworld*.

INTRODUCTION

✦ ✦ ✦

As a boy, London was like a fairy-tale city to me. The other
tenants in my house (apart from us eight kids and my parents)
were a female spy, a fading actress, a newly arrived Irish family
and the mysterious Miss White, a Dickensian spinster. In Earls
Court Road I remember a grocer's shop where the queue included
Arab women in burqas and a beautiful transvestite. My father
helped the women work out their change using his wartime
Arabic. The local sweet shop was run by Pathans. I used to walk
for hours randomly across London and it never disappointed:
I found India in Southall High Road, and old Beirut in Edgware
Road by night. Reggae throbbed in Notting Hill and Kilburn
pubs resounded to Irish freedom songs. The marching music of
the Changing of the Guard gave me goosebumps. I remember
a Sherlock Holmes-style 'pea-souper' fog, and the silence of
Churchill's funeral. History was all around in such a way that
I got temporal vertigo, that sensation of suddenly seeing the past
as a reality. Walking to school I would mentally spool back to see
dinosaurs lumbering down Kensington High Street.

The Victorian historian Macaulay imagined an artist from New
Zealand sitting on a broken arch of London Bridge, sketching
the ruins of London. What if that artist asked what the city was
like? You could give him a pile of facts, but he might get a better

idea if you were to open a magic casement or two onto different moments of London's past. That is what I have tried to do.

You can read this book in any order, or leave it in the lavatory for the occasional reverie. It is neither guide book nor conventional history. In *A Passage to India*, Forster says of Aziz, 'yes, it was all true of him but somehow his essence was slain'. London, like Aziz, cannot be encapsulated. To Shelley it was 'that great sea that still howls for more', and Charles Lamb 'often shed tears in the motley Strand for fullness of joy at so much life'. Carlyle, in a mile-high balloon basket in 1863, swore he could hear London's strange music, a sort of composite sigh.

Writers feature prominently. It is an inky city, a capital of books more than any city in the world. From Chaucer to Dickens, you can hear the saltiness of London speech. Music made in London also has a London stamp, from Purcell and Handel to The Kinks and The Clash. London has rocked the world and the three-note beat preceding the words 'We Will Rock You' was first stamped out by Brian May almost by accident on the wooden floor of a North London church hall.

It is also a city of extraordinary silences. It is a commercial hub full of philosophers and meditators, a roaring place where suddenly you can turn, as Dickens did, into Wardrobe Place and hear only chirping sparrows echoing on old stones. Places like Kensal Green Cemetery, Holland Park and Rainham Marshes are ancient country, which, unlike much of Britain, have never been sprayed with chemicals. To stop rowing on the mighty Thames and simply glide along is mystically calming.

Londoners love their history but this alchemical city does not get weighed down by it too much. A blue plaque in Camden reads 'On this site in 1782 nothing happened'.

LON
DIN
IVM

ANCIENT LONDON

SINGING NEANDERTHAL LONDONERS

✦ ✦ ✦

L ondon has been occupied for 500,000 years: Neanderthal man dropped stone tools near Waterloo Station, east of Richmond Bridge and close to the Sikh temple in Woolwich. A particularly fine hand axe from 400,000 BC, now in the Museum of London, was found near St Paul's Cathedral. Archaeologists have refined the Neanderthal's caveman reputation: yes, he was bull-headed and low-browed, and his 'close encounter' hunting style gave him as many injuries as a rodeo rider, but he was no grunting orc.

His communication was often more sophisticated than our jabbering, for, although language had yet to evolve, he used 'musilanguage', a singing communication. Tone of voice is still perhaps more important between us than the words used; even dogs react to our intonation and tone – our musilanguage – more than to our words. So the first Londoners can be imagined – tall and athletic, hunting in groups and intoning to each other with expressive hand gestures and facial expressions. They laughed as well, for that activity, like singing, predated words. The recent eyebrow-raising discovery that modern man had sex and subsequent progeny with these singing Neanderthals makes them intimately part of modern London.[1]

They were immigrants, of course, descendants of the 'bipedal hominids', as archaeologists romantically call early prototypes of man, who arrived, via Europe, from Kenya a million years ago. They flooded in unchecked roughly along the route of the current A2 from Dover (see box), a chalk ridge which is Britain's oldest highway (the English Channel is only 400,000 years old).

> Charles Dickens's character David Copperfield walked the route in the other direction from London, to stay with the eccentric Betsey Trotwood on the Kent coast. Dickens had an eye for such temporal vertigo: one muddy day he suddenly imagined a pre-Neanderthal London and saw 'a Megalosaurus, forty feet long or so, waddling like an elephantine lizard up Holborn Hill'.

Notes

1. See Stephen Mithen, *The Singing Neanderthals* (Weidenfeld and Nicolson, 2005); Ewen Callaway, 'Mystery Humans Spiced Up Ancients' Sex Lives', *Nature* (19 November 2013).

MINDFUL WALKING AT TERMINAL FIVE

✦ ✦ ✦

Deep in the forest 32km (20 miles) from Warsaw is a granite boulder recording the death, in 1627, of the last auroch. Fossils from India show that aurochs roamed the earth two million years ago. We mostly know them from the marvellous Lascaux cave paintings in France, which show the bulls with their 76cm (30in) forward-pointing horns, rich chestnut coats and white spinal stripe. The skull of the Polish beast – a spinster auroch who died naturally – was stolen by invading Swedish troops and is now in Stockholm Museum. These Tolkienesque beasts weighed a tonne. Eyewitness accounts are tremulous.

PREHISTORIC LONDONERS

Scroll forward to Holloway Lane, a busy road north of Heathrow and west of Southall. It has some listed artisans' houses, and, being near the airport, plenty of car-hire firms. Here, in 1800 BC, in a warm and wooded London, hunters killed a large auroch and cut it up for food. It took six arrows to kill it and, when archaeologists studied the flint arrowheads in 1985, they found traces of animal fat and, to lubricate entry, beeswax.

This area, the London borough of Hillingdon, with its large and friendly Indian population (and Border Agency detention blocks), was a major site in prehistoric times. Just north of Holloway Lane, in Uxbridge, reindeer and horses were butchered in a settlement that lasted for thousands of years. The Uxbridge camps were

carefully sited to intercept the annual reindeer migration up the Thames Valley.

These early Londoners favoured higher ground. Much of the London area was marshy alongside the Thames, which was not embanked. This was fine for the many beavers and hippos that lived there but, at Upminster in the east (on the modern District Line), both a young elephant and a woolly mammoth got stuck in swampland and died of starvation. So Hampstead Heath, then as now, was popular with humanity; many campfire hearths have been found there, with thousands of flint tools dating back to 7000 BC. Over at King's Cross, a mammoth was killed. The skeleton, with the hand axe used to butcher it, was found in 1690 – one of the earliest realizations of London's exotic prehistoric past. With flint factories discovered at Southwark and Woolwich, a 1500 BC jetty at Vauxhall and evidence of contemporary wooden buildings at Westminster and Waterloo, it now seems arbitrary to see London as a Roman invention.

THESE PRE-ROMAN LONDONERS, LIVING AT THE SAME TIME AS STONEHENGE WAS ERECTED, WERE LIKE MODERN LONDONERS IN MANY WAYS. THEY LEFT A LOT OF RUBBISH, THEY DRANK A LOT OF BOOZE AND THEY WERE CULINARILY ADVENTUROUS.

These pre-Roman Londoners, living at the same time as Stonehenge was erected, were like modern Londoners in many ways. They left a lot of rubbish, they drank a lot of booze and they were culinarily adventurous. But what of their spiritual life? This is a mystery, but London does possess one of the most suggestive of all structures from the period: at Heathrow there is a cursus – a long, straight track with raised earth banks on either side – constructed in about 3000 BC.

THE HEATHROW CURSUS

Stonehenge has the other major cursus in Britain, which in 2007 was dated to 3600 BC. It is over 3.2km (2 miles) long and 91.5m (100yd) wide. The Heathrow cursus was first spotted in 1943 from the air. It is so long, straight and flat – 4km (2½ miles) long and 18.25m (20yd) wide – that it was thought to be a Roman road. The construction of Terminal Five, although unpopular with local residents, was a chance to study it. This seven-year operation became the biggest dig ever conducted in Britain. A total of 80,000 objects were found, including a ritually important worked stone from Cornwall and the only wooden bowl known from the Bronze Age: romantic finds from a dig which centred on the wonderfully named Perry Oaks Sludge Works.

Traces of a large roundhouse, too big to be a residence, confirmed the ritual importance of this sacred landscape, but what was the ritual? Archaeologists are victims of their era. Victorians, muscularly Christian, saw human sacrifice and barbarity at Stonehenge; the 'slaughter stone' there is their nomenclature. Current orthodoxy leans towards Stonehenge being an internationally important healing centre. The cursus links sacred sites there, and surely this explains the Heathrow cursus, rather than the gauntlet-running theory that goes back to William Stukeley, the eighteenth-century historian who thought up the name 'cursus', or 'racetrack'.

It was a processional way, aligned on the winter sunset, for the sort of meditative walking that is a human need: consider the circumambulations of Mount Kailash by Hindus or of stupas by Buddhists, or the walking of cloisters by monks. Indeed, many of us like to think things over during a solitary walk. The Latin term *Solvitur ambulando* means 'By walking it is solved'.

FROM CURSUS TO TRAVELATOR

The holidays that begin at Heathrow are not unlike an ancient cathartic ceremony, so I think that if the builders of the cursus were transported through time they would understand the functions of the airport once they had got over the shock of the existence of aeroplanes. The way that airport visitors display physical affection would not surprise them either. In Terminal Five they would also find the only 'temple' in London congenial to their lost beliefs: the prayer room run by the Heathrow chaplaincy, whose mission is 'to minister to those of all faiths and none, to be a non-anxious presence in stressful times and to

> I THINK THAT IF THE BUILDERS OF THE CURSUS WERE TRANSPORTED THROUGH TIME THEY WOULD UNDERSTAND THE FUNCTIONS OF THE AIRPORT ONCE THEY HAD GOT OVER THE SHOCK OF THE EXISTENCE OF AEROPLANES.

encourage social cohesion'. This is probably what the cursus builders were all about too: the dig report concludes that the Heathrow community of 3000 BC was 'a more stable and equitable society' than anywhere else in the south-east, and explains that the cursus would have 'bonded the inhabitants of the area in a spirit of shared purpose'.[1]

Empire of the Sun author J. G. Ballard, a lover of London fringe-lands and of airports, lived at Shepperton, near Heathrow. He wrote that 'We're all looking for a vertical route out of the concrete jungle we're living in.' In a 1997 essay called 'Airports: Cities of the Future', he praises their egalitarian ethos and 'easy camaraderie'. At Heathrow, he points out, nostalgia and kitsch are absent ('I have never seen a pebble-dashed Control Tower') and everyone briefly becomes a world citizen.[2] Bulldoze the gentrified stucco terraces of London, he suggests. Mankind, he says, is truly happy at the check-in desk, in transit to a better state of being – like the person, I suggest, at one end of the cursus. The excited travellers gliding along the travelators of Terminal Five are the direct successors of prehistoric walkers. So, whether it is the mysterious civilization of the Heathrow sacred landscape, or the airport itself, Heathrow shows us an alternative London, a launch pad for the psyche.

It is good to end on a mystery. Every cursus in the country has one embankment higher than the other. Why? Nobody knows.

Notes

1. 'Archaeology at Terminal Five', available on the official Heathrow Airport website. The site has a nice animation of crowds on the cursus observing the sunrise at winter solstice.
2. 'Airports: Cities of the Future', *Blueprint* September 1997. See also *Prehistoric Avenues and Alignments* (English Heritage, 2011) and Christopher Chippindale's *Stonehenge Complete* (Thames and Hudson, 2012).

ROMANS IN ECSTASY, AD 240–350

✦ ✦ ✦

The excavation of London's Roman Temple of Mithras, discovered during rebuilding work in 1954, was an exciting time for a 49-year-old Welshman called William Grimes. Grimes, the son of a draughtsman in Pembroke docks, was the director of the Museum of London and became an overnight celebrity, with his flaming red hair and trademark red carnation buttonhole. After a superb head of Mithras was found on the last day allowed by developers for the dig, a parliamentary debate was held: a motion was passed to continue the excavation.

Not only was the temple archaeologically sensational, with the finest Roman sculptures found in Britain, but Grimes worked on the dig with an older woman called Audrey Williams. Grimes and Audrey, a feisty Oxford graduate who had already married twice, fell in love. The archaeologist divorced his childhood sweetheart Barbara – the mother of his two children – and married Audrey in 1959. Making a clean break with William's past, Audrey renamed him Peter, after the contemporary Britten opera, much to his colleagues' irritation. After Audrey's death the priapic Grimes, at 76, married the youngish Molly Douglas (aged 54). Poor old Molly: Grimes's ashes were to be buried with Audrey's.

The temple floor can still be seen in the bustling financial heart of the City: you can go there and allow it to take you on a mental journey to an ancient world of pagan gods. For here were conducted the most extraordinary rituals ever seen in London – rituals rooted in the minds of cave-painting man.

MITHRAS

Mithras (Mitra in ancient India and Mesopotamia) was worshipped as a god of friendship, constancy and courage. The cult flourished in ancient Iran, surviving into Roman times among Turkish pirates; after the Roman emperor had settled the pirates in Calabria, southern Italy, it soon spread to Rome.

Mithraism, a secretive cult, remains mysterious. Its practices are only known from a few scraps of papyrus, a vase painting in Mainz, Germany, frescoes in other Mithras temples, and from two early Christian accounts, written when the cult was being suppressed. It was the most popular religion among Roman soldiers, and there are Mithras temples, or Mithrea, all over the ancient world – from Spain to Syria, from Iraq to Bagram in Afghanistan, and of course in Rome, which has over 600. A rare Roman poem about a Mithraeum begins:

This is the place, auspicious and sacred, holy and favourable.[1]

INSIDE THE MITHRAEUM

London's Mithraeum was carefully sited next to the Walbrook stream. Fresh water was needed and the Walbrook – 'stream of the Britons' – was inhabited by water spirits. Offerings have been found on the old stream bed, including a lead oblong with a woman's name written backwards, as a way of cursing her. But the site was marshy – even in 1954

OFFERINGS HAVE BEEN FOUND ON THE OLD STREAM BED, INCLUDING A LEAD OBLONG WITH A WOMAN'S NAME WRITTEN BACKWARDS, AS A WAY OF CURSING HER.

Grimes battled with water just 1.2m (4ft) down – so the buttresses of the 18.25 x 6m (60 x 20ft) temple were massive and deep.

All the temples to Mithras have the same format, being built to look, from within, like caves – and so are windowless. Ceilings were usually painted as dark blue star charts. Initiates were handed a sacred drink by a man wearing a mask depicting a raven's head and went through seven stages, emulating different beasts. (In a throwback to Mithraism's ancient roots, loose trousers were worn; Romans usually saw trousers as barbaric.) St Jerome (AD 347–420) said that they flapped their arms like birds and roared like lions, but recent scholarship is less dismissive; the whole religion seems to have been aimed at inducing, through guided breathing exercises and a psycho-dramatic rebirth, a profound happiness, beloved of Socrates, called *eudaimonia*. It sounds crazy, but is perhaps no crazier than any modern religion, baldly described.

The London Mithraeum went out of fashion in about AD 250, but fortunately for us, its sculptures were carefully buried under the floor. They are now in the Museum of London. With the pragmatism typical of Londoners, the building became a temple to Bacchus for a while before it gently subsided back into the marshy ground, about 700 years before the Tower of London was built.

So, hard by the mayor's Mansion House with its stifling ceremonial, and the Bank of England with its liveried flunkies, was a sunken cave-temple where, for over a century, Romans descended in search of an ancient ecstasy.

Note

1. Jonas Bjornebye, *The Cult of Mithras,* Ph.D. thesis, University of Bergen, Norway, 2007. Having read this dense study I feel, like Jonas, very grateful to Felix and Pio, his two sons, who were born during the writing and had to vie with the lure of an ancient deity for their father's time. J. North and S. Price's *The Religious History of the Roman Empire* (Oxford University Press, 2011) explodes many myths about Mithras being a Roman invention, and reinstates the role of women in Mithraism (pp.260–63). You would never guess at Grimes's raffish ways from the magisterial tone of his dig write-up in *Recent Archaeological Excavations,* edited by R. L. S. Bruce-Mitford (Routledge, 1956), a book worth seeing for the wonderful paintings of the temple in its marshy London setting, complete with raven-headed men.

MEDIEVAL LONDON

FAIRIES IN LONDON

✦ ✦ ✦

Surprisingly, London is the worldwide hotspot for fairy sightings and fairy lore. Tudor times were the high tide of fairy beliefs, but our little friends stayed around right up to modern times. Fairies are the successors of the ancient water nymphs and woodland spirits (such as fauns and dryads) that Christianity drove underground into so-called folklore. As the Londoner Geoffrey Chaucer put it, holy friars' prayers frightened away the fairies. Shakespeare's fairy king, Oberon, was a tougher sprite and boasted of not being frightened by church bells.

Academics have not flocked to fairy studies, and are puzzled by Shakespeare's interest in them. They routinely suggest that the passage in *Romeo and Juliet* in which Mercutio describes a fairy carriage in hallucinogenic detail must be a passage inserted by another writer. More likely, perhaps, Shakespeare was merely reflecting common beliefs and a contemporary fascination. One of his heroes, Smithfield lad Edmund Spenser, wrote the epic twelve-book poem *The Faerie Queen*. (Spenser died in 1599 aged 46. At his funeral in Westminster Abbey, his fellow poets threw unpublished poems into his grave.)

As the revered historian Keith Thomas admits in his definitive study on religion and magic, 'In Elizabethan times fairy lore was accepted literally at a popular level.' In London, food and water were often left out for fairies, just as modern children leave food for Santa's reindeer.[1]

Fairies could be mischievous, but were useful household deities. They pinched would-be adulterers. Maids, upon spilling milk, would say: 'Robin jogged me' (Robin Goodfellow was the Artful Dodger of fairies). Waking up with tangled hair, or elf-locks, was evidence of fairies at play and if cutlery disappeared, fairies had borrowed it, a nicely stress-free way to deal with such losses. As Westminster poet Robert Herrick said in 1631, fairies had a moral code, 'a mixt religion part pagan part papist'.

Two London court cases shed incidental light on fairy beliefs in the capital. In 1595, Judith Phillips was whipped through the City for extracting money from the public with the promise of meeting the Queen of the Fairies. Sir Anthony Ashley was more ambitious. In 1610 he was fined for extortion on multiple counts; he had been taking money from 'dupes' by promising that he could arrange for them to marry the Queen of the Fairies.

THE FIRST LORD OF THE ADMIRALTY, GOODWIN WHARTON MP, WAS AN UNUSUALLY HIGH-PROFILE FAIRY-BELIEVER, WHO IN 1688 PURSUED THEIR TREASURE UNDER SOMERSET HOUSE IN THE STRAND, BUT ONLY SUCCEEDED IN UNLEASHING FOUR DEVILS, ONE OF WHOM SHOT OUT OF THE WINDOW AND OVER THE THAMES 'WITH A HISS'.

The First Lord of the Admiralty, Goodwin Wharton MP, was an unusually high-profile fairy-believer, who in 1688 pursued their treasure under Somerset House in the Strand, but only succeeded in unleashing four devils, one of whom shot out of the window and over the Thames 'with a hiss'. At Wharton's next excavation, under a house in Holborn, nothing was found but not, he felt, because nothing was there: he left a £50 tip for the fairies. When Wharton's lover complained of his lack of sexual arousal, he explained that he was exhausted: the Queen of the Fairies had engaged in vigorous sex with him as he slept.

BELIEFS DURING THE ENLIGHTENMENT

Even at the heart of eighteenth-century London, an interest in fairies lingered. Several Royal Society members, including British Museum founder Sir Hans Sloane and George Graham, inventor of the mercury pendulum, formed the occult Cabala Club, which met upstairs at the Sun Tavern next to St Paul's churchyard. A founder club member, John Byrom, possessed written invocations to summon up 'the Queen of the Pharies'.

A London notable who went public with his belief in fairies was Regency scientist Sir Humphry Davy, lecturer in chemistry at the Royal Institution and the discoverer of several elements. He described fairies' wings in detail, and their cosmic hangout on Saturn. Davy's friend Samuel Taylor Coleridge once reflected that he could never be really close to Wordsworth because the Lakeland bard did not believe in fairies. As Coleridge put it, 'We cannot live on matter-of-factness alone.' As with Shakespeare, Coleridge knew that the fairy realm was a way to access inwardness and the wisdom of the unconscious.

> SAMUEL TAYLOR COLERIDGE ONCE REFLECTED THAT HE COULD NEVER BE REALLY CLOSE TO WORDSWORTH BECAUSE THE LAKELAND BARD DID NOT BELIEVE IN FAIRIES. AS COLERIDGE PUT IT, 'WE CANNOT LIVE ON MATTER-OF-FACTNESS ALONE'.

Wordsworth described his contemporary, the Soho poet William Blake, as completely mad. This was a common opinion, but Blake's mysticism is now more widely appreciated. As Peter Ackroyd has pointed out, Blake never left London for any significant period, even when offered a free tour of Europe, preferring to sit naked with his wife in his London back garden, accessing the collective unconscious. In London, Blake found portals to other worlds, including fairyland. Sitting at dinner one day as the conversation dragged, he asked the woman sitting next to him, 'And have you ever seen a fairy funeral, madam?' She had not. 'Nor I,' Blake went on, 'until last night, in my back garden.' The mourners were all a soft green, about the size of large grasshoppers, and the deceased fairy was carried on a rose leaf.

TWENTIETH CENTURY

Who embodies rational deductive reasoning? Sherlock Holmes. Remarkably, in 1922 Sir Arthur Conan Doyle of Wimpole Street, just off Oxford Street, wrote *The Coming of the Fairies*, the most definitive defence of real fairies since Robert Kirk's *The Secret Commonwealth of Fairies* (1691). Although the fake 'Cottingley photographs' inspired much of the book, Doyle's work is a comprehensive reference book: English fairies are green, as Blake saw, but in Brittany they are grey-green, in Sicily orange and purple, and in California white and gold. Australia has sky-blue fairies whilst Java is thick with indigo entities. To Doyle, only our rampant commercialism stopped us from seeing fairies as of old. He ended the book by hoping for a future era of 'mutual good feeling' between fairies and humans.

How heart-warmed he would have been about the huge success of Kensington visitors Peter Pan and Tinkerbell. Thanks to

J. M. Barrie, every year thousands of children in theatres shout out their belief in fairies to save Tinkerbell.

And so, dear reader – and I do feel affection for those who have journeyed this far – this chronicle of London fairy lore hits the age of the Blitz, of Woolworth's and of swinging London. Surely this must be the end of fairies in London? No. Curiously, on a gas-lit street connecting Notting Hill and Kensington High Street, a garden that was inhabited by real fairies, one of whom has become famous, survived until 1966. This was the garden of a painter, Estella Canziani, who died in 1964.[2] She saw fairies in the garden and kept it wild for them. Her painting of one sitting against a tree trunk, *The Piper of Dreams*, has struck such a chord with humanity that Conan Doyle would indeed have been pleased. It is even more popular than Holman Hunt's *Light of the World*, that great Jesus portrait. Millions of Pipers adorn greetings cards.

AN ARTIST'S GARDEN

I was born at home on the other side of Kensington High Street in 1955, the seventh of eight children. Many of my siblings remember Estella Canziani painting in Holland Park or out for

a stroll, dressed in the style of the 1920s. I think I remember seeing her ... I want to.

My father, a cockney water diviner who knew Canziani well, took us all on a walk every Sunday morning on the same route at the same time. He had been a regimental sergeant major, you see. The walk went past Canziani's garden and that was always the magical part. It was so thickly overgrown that, try as I might – and I tried every Sunday – I could hardly glimpse the warm red brick of Canziani's eighteenth-century house. (It had been built as Queen Anne's laundry for Kensington Palace over the road.)

As I grew older, the foliage just grew thicker, and I became less passionate about peering through the hedge for fleeting fairies. Canziani died in 1964 and when I was 11, the house was demolished. On a Sunday morning walk my dad took us through the fence and into the demolition site. The house was almost gone and most of the garden was wrecked and churned up by demolition vehicles. But he wanted to show us the old mulberry tree, which was still there. Canziani, who had lived there for over 60 years, since Victorian times, had told my father that the tree had provided fruit for the palace in the eighteenth century, which seemed very likely from the girth of its trunk.

A few days later, the tree was destroyed. Modern flats went up on the site. The garden is car-parking space now, so London's fairies must live in other wild gardens around the capital, and perhaps in magical wooded Holland Park nearby, which Canziani loved.

Notes

1. Keith Thomas, *Religion and the Decline of Magic*, studies in popular belief in sixteenth- and seventeenth-century England (Weidenfeld and Nicolson, 1971), p.726.
2. Estella Canziani, *Round About Three Palace Green* (Methuen, 1939).

HALL OF THE PEOPLE, 1097

✦ ✦ ✦

Most people are unaware that, buried amid the jumble of the Victorian Parliament buildings is a hall which should be as famous as the Great Mosque in Istanbul. Westminster Hall, which at 76m (250ft) long is only a few feet shorter than that mosque, was the greatest achievement of medieval secular architecture in Europe, and the largest hall in the medieval world.

Until recently, a single-span, unsupported roof for this 21m-wide (70ft) structure was deemed beyond eleventh-century abilities. For centuries, antiquarians grubbed around in the floor for the column bases that would solve the mystery of this prodigious space. Finding none, they presumed that there had been wooden columns, which had rotted away. More sophisticated modern research has proved that, in 1097, the largest unsupported roof in the world was built. We will never know how. (Nor do we yet know the identity of a holy man who was buried in the walls standing up, in a linen shroud and with a crozier.)

Even the later thirteenth-century hammer-beam roof of today is a wonder of the world, the finest medieval carpentry on the planet, patched as it is with man-of-war timbers from Nelson's time. A recent restorer who worked up there said it was 'like being in some primeval forest', so massive and complex were the sturdy oak beams.

When the hall was finished, it stood alone in splendour by the river with its 1.8m-thick (6ft) walls and massive flying buttresses. Smoke issued from a central hole in the roof, Viking-style – there was no chimney. The walls were chequered with golden Caen stone and grey-green Reigate stone, a patchwork to symbolize one harmonious kingdom, France and Britain united. It must have been the pride of London in 1097 (see box).

If you believe in 'tides in the affairs of men', contemporary China was in its Song Dynasty golden age, in Africa the huge capital of Great Zimbabwe was under construction, Islam was entering its Cordoban era of splendour, and King Chola in southern India was giving land to 'untouchables' whilst making peace with China and Cambodia. In western India, Vikramaditya was a Hindu William Rufus, loving song, poetry and building.

WILLIAM RUFUS

The man responsible for the hall has been similarly hidden
from view. King William II (c.1056–1100), commonly known as
William Rufus, was an easily bored maverick with an innovative
intelligence. Impatient with the wealth of a bloated and corrupt
Church, he fleeced it efficiently, refused to support the Crusades,
banned the church courts' ridiculous 'ordeal by hot iron',
and appointed a genuine mystic, St Anselm, as Archbishop of
Canterbury. William's homosexuality cast a longer shadow over
his name – gay relationships were illegal in England and Wales
until 1967. Medieval chroniclers, mostly churchmen, gave him
a bad press and blamed his death at about 40, in a hunting
accident, on divine retribution. Over the homophobic centuries,
historians, a pallid and literal-minded breed, have missed his
jokes and trashed his reputation.

Imagine the king – with long, blond hair and the ruddy face
that gave him his nickname. Anselm affectionately called him
'the wild bull'. The absurdities of relic worship, which Chaucer
had yet to satirize, account for William's amusing habitual
imprecation: 'By the Holy Face of Lucca!' (see box). Bitter monks
and po-faced academics have quoted his reaction to being bought
shoes which cost a shilling as evidence
of his vanity, but the context makes
clear that the words 'Am I the son of a
whore that you bring me cheap shoes?'
was not a serious rant.

> The Holy Face of Lucca
> is a venerated wooden
> figure said to have been
> carved by Joseph of
> Arimathen.

His funny comment to someone who
marvelled at his hall – 'It's just a
bedchamber compared to the size
I really wanted' – has been taken as somehow power-mad. But
the stutter-prone William, unlike the chroniclers, could not take

himself too seriously, and his foremost biographer detected that 'even monastic writers could not conceal their delight' at his ways.[1] He was a dandy who loved any fashion craze and even wore long, curling 'scorpion's tail' shoes, but he was also an accomplished soldier and hunter, a macho man. He held on to a united kingdom and, startlingly, modern Arthurian scholarship has tracked the ideal of King Arthur to this raffish medieval Johnny Depp.

A HUGE SPACE

This brings us back to another mystery about the hall, one that no historian has answered. What was it for, and why did William want it to be so huge? Its later use as courtroom and a place for Mandela and Obama to make speeches gives a clue, as does William's Viking descent. His father William the Conqueror was the heir of Hrolfr, leader of the Northmen who invaded Normandy, or 'Norse Land'.

William Rufus wanted a huge, Viking-style moot hall, a place where an almost democratic number of people could meet to debate and agree on a better future. There are ancient moot halls left at Aldeburgh, Suffolk and Fordwich, Kent, and a 'moot point' means not an uncertainty, but something that needs to be postponed for the moot. In true Viking/ medieval style, such a meeting

THERE ARE ANCIENT MOOT HALLS LEFT AT ALDEBURGH, SUFFOLK AND FORDWICH, KENT, AND A 'MOOT POINT' MEANS NOT AN UNCERTAINTY, BUT SOMETHING THAT NEEDS TO BE POSTPONED FOR THE MOOT.

would often include a feast. Music would be in evidence, and William was a friend of the great French troubadour singer the

Duke of Aquitaine. Inside, as plaster fragments attest, the hall was painted in glowing colours.

Throughout the Middle Ages, knights did assemble there to argue their rights, often in full armour. In 1250 Londoners en masse threatened rebellion and Henry III tearfully came to an agreement with them. On several occasions the poor were invited in to huge feasts: 6,000 people slept and fed in the hall from Christmas Eve 1237 until 2 January.

Although much pompous ceremony took over the hall, the space has retained, psycho-geographically, an atmosphere of revolutionary change.

TRIALS, TAVERNS AND TENNIS

William Rufus would have smiled at an invasion by hundreds of Londoners in 1640, demanding the abolition of bishops. Here Charles I was tried, and Cromwell installed as head of state. Here the tears of Devon girl Elizabeth Chudleigh melted the judges' hearts. Found guilty of bigamy, they let her off the punishment of branding on the hand. Soldiers at the door shouted much of the trial, line by line, to the huge crowd outside.

Charles James Fox understood William's vision for the space when he rallied over 3,000 people there to oppose a coal tax. So did John Wilkes, who filled the place in 1769 with a mob demanding the dissolution of Parliament.

And here, in 1788, British imperialism was put on trial, as Warren Hastings, Governor-General of Bengal, faced a seven-year impeachment for peculation. The prosecutor was the philosopher

Edmund Burke, who spoke 'on behalf of the millions of India'. His nine-day-long speech became a bestselling book and remains a classic hatchet job on imperialists.

Atheists were finally allowed in the Commons soon after Charles Bradlaugh, MP filled the hall with a protest meeting against an antiquated prohibition.

Perhaps dearest to William's own affections, two popular young gay men – known on account of their cross-dressing theatre act as Fanny and Stella – were tried and released in 1871: the court found that transvestism was not a criminal act, just fun.

Fun was a thread in the hall's life too, from medieval jousting to the two busy taverns known as Heaven and Hell at the end of the building – named from their old identity as prison cells. Ben Jonson's play *The Alchemist* mentions Heaven, and Pepys records an evening carousing there with the composer Purcell. In 1920, two Tudor tennis balls were found in the hall's roof beams.

Today the hall, with its gift shop and heavy security, seems tamer but its spirit lives in the walls; only recently a fine old dagger in a fleur-de-lys sheath was found jammed into a crevice.

Notes
1. Frank Barlow, *William Rufus* (Yale University Press, 2000), p.219.

THE JESTER AND
THE HOSPITAL, 1123

✦ ✦ ✦

S t Bartholomew's Hospital – 'Bart's' – is a world-famous
teaching hospital just north of the City, in Smithfield. It has
pioneered both the X-ray (1896) and radiotherapy (1937).
Its staff have included William Harvey, who discovered the
circulation of the blood, Ethel Manson, the first female registered
nurse, and Dr Watson, assistant of Sherlock Holmes. Nowadays it
has a multimillion-pound budget and a five-year plan to become
'a healthcare platform committed to relentless improvement'.

Bart's is the oldest hospital in the world, and has been looking
after Londoners for nearly 1,000 years. The whole operation was
founded by a twelfth-century jester called Rahere, and on the
fifth floor, Ward 5B is named after him. Like many clowns, he
never used a surname. A man 'of low lineage', he inveigled his
way into court life 'with japes and flattery'. He was a cockney
wide boy, firmly in the tradition of Max Miller and Michael
Caine. The court of Henry I was a heady place. The black-haired
king, stocky and barrel-chested, worked and played hard, had
many mistresses and loved the arts, especially music. Rahere
was sometimes described as a minstrel, so perhaps his music first

gained him access to court. Once there, he certainly participated fully in the revels.

RAHERE'S PILGRIMAGE

'Suddenly' – to quote the life story written a few years after his death – Rahere felt the need for penance, for a pilgrimage to Rome. This seems in line with his mercurial personality. He may have gone alone and had no entourage caring for him when he caught malarial fever in the papal city. He vowed that, if he recovered, he would found a hospital for the poor in Smithfield on his return. Why Smithfield? 'Smoothfield', as it was originally known, was an open, flat, elevated area north of the crowded city, popular as a jousting field. Rahere recovered and, on his way home, had a vision of St Bartholomew, an apostle associated with healing.

On Rahere's return, his courtier friends told him of a potential snag: the king owned Smithfield and it could not be built on without royal permission. But Henry, who himself became increasingly pious as he grew older, remembered his old jester and agreed. The Bishop of London blessed the land and, with Church support, Rahere founded both the hospital and a monastery church to serve it. He became a monk, and served as both prior and master of the hospital.

ST BARTHOLOMEW THE GREAT

The church Rahere founded, St Bartholomew the Great, remains and with its massive Norman nave, it is one of London's three surviving complete early medieval churches, the other two being the Tower of London chapel and the Dan-Brown-friendly Temple Church off the Strand. Rahere's tomb, with its colourful effigy of Rahere, is in the church.

Rahere's monks were proud of their foundation, and especially of the Chapel of Our Lady. One of them was Hubert, an old monk of 'wonderful gentleness', who had 'escaped naked from the wreckage of this world', i.e. given away all his possessions to become a monk. Hubert loved praying for long periods in the Lady chapel, a place which gradually became neglected in favour of services in the main church. One day, when Hubert was praying alone in the chapel, the Virgin Mary appeared to him. She had come down, she said, from *sumo celorum cardine* – basically, the portals of heaven. A veritable chatterbox, she spoke at length and with 'honeyed lips' about how her blessings would descend on the chapel if more monks prayed there. Many miracles of healing happened thereafter at the church, mirroring the medical work at the hospital next door. Although the chapel was absorbed into a house and used as a coal cellar during the Reformation, it is now restored.[1]

Rahere died in *c*.1143, but his monks retained an independent spirit. In 1247 the Archbishop of Canterbury, Boniface, was outraged by their lack of deference to him. Boniface, from Provence, was both the son of a French count and the Queen's uncle. Entering the church in full armour, he slapped a monk in the face, tore off his robes and crushed the cleric against a pillar. Other monks ejected the fiery archbishop from the church, and complained to the Pope about his unholy conduct. Boniface left England for a while but, with his connections, he soon returned to be archbishop until 1270.

St Bartholomew's is an atmospheric church, dark and cavernous, and two tombs in particular seem to preserve Rahere's irreverent jesting style: firstly, John Whiting's touching epitaph near the altar:

> *She first deceased, he for a little tried*
> *To live without her, lik'd it not, and dy'd*

and secondly, the monument to philosopher Edward Cooke, made of a marble that drips in damp weather. The inscription enjoins the passer-by to weep:

> *Unsluice, ye briny floods. What? Can ye keep*
> *your eyes from tears and see the marble weep?*

800 years after Rahere another British humorist, Blackadder co-creator Richard Curtis, came to the jester's church to film *Four Weddings and a Funeral*. I have repeatedly thought during the writing of this book: there seems to be something in the *genius loci* idea – spirit of place, or as it is less romantically called, psychogeography. Maybe buildings have memories.

BLOODY NEIGHBOURS

The buildings of Bart's, opposite Smithfield meat market, are unique and evocative: John Betjeman, who lived overlooking the churchyard, loved the way white-coated doctors mingled on the square with bloody-coated meat porters.

Note
1. *Records of St Bartholomew's Priory and Church* by E. A. Webb (2 vols., Oxford University Press, 1921); Augustus Hare's *Walks in London, Volume 1* (1878), pp.180–90, is enjoyable.

TUDOR LONDON

THE EMPIRE THAT STARTED IN A TAVERN

✦ ✦ ✦

One evening in 1598 at the Nag's Head Tavern, while Shakespeare was probably drinking nearby at the Mermaid, or at home in Blackfriars writing, a few merchants agreed to found what became the East India Company (EIC). This extraordinary corporation eventually held sway over millions of Indians, was the greatest commercial enterprise in the world, and was London's biggest civilian employer. According to *The Economist* in 2013, the EIC 'spawned Company Man'.

By the nineteenth century, the EIC, or 'John Company', had its own army of 200,000 men and a navy, the 'Bombay Marine', with sailing ships built at its own London shipyards. These ships, known as East Indiamen, were of such enviable quality that the Royal Navy routinely bought them second-hand, especially after the company pioneered the steamship.

EXOTIC GOODS

Company warehouses, mostly six storeys high, covered 2.8 hectares (7 acres) of the City and dockland, served by a fleet of horse-drawn carts. The warehouses stored not just tea but also vermicelli, silk, tamarind, saffron and a medicinal bark called sassafras. There was iris root for perfumes, lapis lazuli for jewellery and orchal, a dye made from Indian lichen. The warehouse inventories are poetry: madder and cochineal, sarsaparilla and camphor (see box). There were cassia buds, which were laxatives, and nux vomica – poisonous seeds to induce vomiting. One list starts: 'Acorns, agates, aloes, alum, amber, aquafortis, arrangoes' (see box).

Madder is the root extract of a herb, used as a magenta dye. Cochineal is red dye extracted from a winged insect. Sarsaparilla is a preparation of dried rhizomes, used to make the root beer beloved of Calamity Jane, while camphor – the word is Sanskrit – is an effective anaesthetic.

Alum is a water-purifying mineral and anti-coagulant. It was used, in pencil form, to stop small wounds bleeding. Aquafortis is dilute nitric acid. It was used in alchemy, but also to etch letters and patterns on to brass plates and leather bookbindings. Arrangoes are gemstone beads.

There was scammony, a tapeworm-killing root resin from Orissa, and the warehouse stored cowrie shells, feathers, fossils and ginseng (tortoiseshell and sandalwood were kept on the top floor). With the coconuts were kept a dried berry called 'cocculus indicus', which mysteriously increased beer strength. Orange water was in glass jars nearby.

EAST INDIA HOUSE

Overseas royalty were regularly taken on a tour of the Company's London operations. For over 200 years, from 1638 until 1858, the EIC was based at East India House in Leadenhall Street (the site is now the futuristic Lloyds Building, designed by Richard 'Pompidou Centre' Rogers). In 1858, after the Indian Mutiny, the EIC was abruptly disbanded when the Government took over the administration of EIC territories in India. East India House was demolished and the company's army and navy were nationalized (see box, opposite). Queen Victoria became Empress of India and so began the Raj.

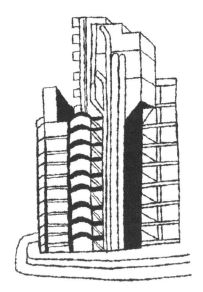

The East India House contents sale included 1,700 doors, hundreds of paintings and Tipu Sultan's dream journal. The Indian galleries at the Victoria and Albert

Museum in Kensington largely consist of the museum from East India House, and several excellent paintings from there adorn the Foreign Office. An unimaginable 305 tonnes (300 tons) of paper records were taken away and pulped, yet millions of manuscript volumes were kept and now comprise a huge department of the British Library: 13km (8 miles) of shelves. One military despatch has 197 attachments, totalling over 13,000 pages.

The EIC's school, Haileybury, had a unique ethos (and is still going). Perhaps it shared the company's toleration of creativity and eccentricity, as later pupils included Kipling and the producer of Monty Python. To train its soldiers, the company set up a large military college in Croydon, near Addiscombe Station. Mostly demolished, the gym is now private housing, but the many Indian street names in Croydon attest to its company days. The military college was so well built that it had to be blown up with dynamite.

OPPRESSOR OR BENEFACTOR?

This long-vanished company still generates heated debate. Some say it was evil: it racked up, for instance, a 32,000 per cent profit on the nutmeg it imported; it supported the opium trade for profit; and worst of all, it ran a sort of empire in India, using its private army to wage war.

And yet, and yet ... the above is a simplification. Racism and evangelical Christianity really only took off in India after the 1858 Crown takeover and the Government-directed brutal suppression of the Indian Mutiny, when memsahibs, missionaries, utilitarians and British army types moved into India en masse. This post-EIC era, the Raj, was the time when British rulers usually horsewhipped servants and eschewed native dress in favour of starch and crinoline. This was also when towns such as Simla were built, replicas of English suburbia. Most films and novels about British India portray this truly imperialist era. In contrast, the EIC made all of its administrators learn Indian languages at the start of their service, before they went near 'the natives'. To educate them about Eastern religion, the company set up its own madrassa, or Islamic college, and a Sanskrit College, in Calcutta.

ASSIMILATION

Company employees in India had generally lived almost like natives, wearing Indian clothes, fasting in Ramadan, marrying Indian wives and often staying in India for over 40 years continuously. EIC employees such as 'Rajasthan' Tod, 'Oriental' Jones and Henry Colebrooke pioneered the study of Sanskrit and Buddhist scriptures, and oversaw the dawn of archaeology in India, discovering and saving thousands of ancient monuments and scriptures. Jones famously wore Indian 'pyjamas' all day and acquired the odd habit of 'shampooing' his hair daily (both words are Hindi).

Elijah Impey was a pioneer collector of Indian art, and his friend Nathaniel Halhed rediscovered and published ancient Hindu legal texts before writing the first Bengali grammar in 1778. Charles 'Hindoo' Stuart bathed daily in the Ganges and wrote to *The Telegraph* urging British women to 'throw away their whalebone corsets' and wear the much more flattering saris. His book, *A Vindication of the Hindoos*, caused a storm. These men have been sidelined by the racist horrors of the later Empire.

AN ENDURING INFLUENCE

The employees of this one London building shook Europe: figures such as Goethe and Schopenhauer were scintillated by the new Asian discoveries and talked of an 'oriental Renaissance' in Europe. In later times of religious hatred, it is good to remember this orientalist company. One senior administrator confided in a letter: 'The sacredness of India haunts me like a passion.' The directors of the East India Company in Leadenhall Street tolerated this low-impact, low-cost attitude, and indeed encouraged it, for they had no Palmerston-style imperial ambitions. They wanted to build friendships with local princes and, basically, protect the company's profit.

This 'informal empire' policy often broke down, and warfare ensued, but this should not obscure the fact that this extraordinary company tried not to run India. The old maxim ran, 'The Flag follows trade', but traders didn't usually want the flag, peace being good for business. In the famous words of the Victorian Londoner John Seeley, 'We acquired our empire in a fit of absence of mind.'

A BENEVOLENT EMPLOYER

The EIC may have spawned company man, but it also pioneered some eccentrically advanced HR policies for its thousands of warehousemen and dockworkers. The first ever redundancy package was devised at East India House in 1833. Generous sick pay and pensions were extended to care for workers' families. When Thomas Trotman was transported to Australia for burglary, the EIC paid his wife a pension for life. Pay was above average for manual work, at 3 shillings per day, and paid regularly – this at a time when the Royal Dockyard paid poorly, in arrears, and partly in kind in the form of wood chips for fuel.

EIC warehouses closed on Sunday and the working day was just six hours, 9am to 3pm. The fact that this included a 30-minute mid-morning 'breakfast break' makes the EIC policy more lenient than EU rules today, which give only a fifteen-minute break in a six-hour shift. Voluntary paid overtime was on offer. The Royal Dockyard's working day for most of the nineteenth century was 6am to 6pm.

Health and safety was advanced: candles were only allowed in padlocked lanterns, all doors and beams were iron, and the company had its own salaried fire brigade, which practised weekly. To control its fleet of carts, plying between docks and warehouses, the company invented something called a speed limit of 4kmph (2½ mph), with a

TO CONTROL ITS FLEET OF CARTS, PLYING BETWEEN DOCKS AND WAREHOUSES, THE COMPANY INVENTED SOMETHING CALLED A SPEED LIMIT OF 4KMPH (2½ MPH), WITH A SCALE OF FINES TO COVER TRANSGRESSIONS ALL THE WAY UP TO A HORSE BREAKING INTO A GALLOP.

scale of fines to cover transgressions all the way up to a horse breaking into a gallop. Carts arriving at a warehouse unloaded directly into a loophole by a pulley mechanism. Anyone injured received lifelong sickness benefit. Company employees from the EIC's army or navy, injured in action, were offered easy clerical jobs for life in its warehouses.

Thus William Whiteway, captured as a gunner's boy by Tipu Sultan and who spent ten years in a dungeon, got a job for life in the Cutler Street warehouse. Edward Sheehan, imprisoned by the Chinese, was given a nice sinecure in a Deptford tea warehouse. Jeremiah Leonard, thrown from the topmast of a company ship in a storm off the Cape of Good Hope, lost his right arm. The company trained him to write left-handed and gave him a job for life in its counting house. Many a modern army veteran might crave such treatment.

The EIC's reaction to staff theft from warehouses was typically individual. Rather than send miscreants to Newgate Prison, a living hell, or hand them over for hanging, its first resort was always to whip the employee for over 91m (100yd) down the ever-busy Seething Lane. Its general policy was 'tempered', meaning that miscreants were given, as best practice, a second chance. A government Labour enquiry noted that rates of misconduct were very low in the company, which it attributed to good pay and the efficiency of the organization; this seemed to command the respect of the employees.

Older company employees did not necessarily feel undervalued; they were known as 'elders' and given enhanced benefits. Death in service triggered a look at the family's background: William Prosser's widow was consequently given a lifelong job as a cleaner in East India House.

Although mental illness in Britain was treated barbarically until recent times, the EIC, at the incredibly early date of 1818, established an in-house asylum, Pembroke House, with pleasant gardens, in leafy Hackney. There, mentally ill employees, rather than being simply locked up as in Bedlam, were pensioned and treated with much understanding by the pioneering Dr Williams and Dr South, full-time employees of East India House. Pembroke House outlasted the company, running up to 1870, when it fed into the development of modern care regimes for the mentally ill.

WRITERS WITH PROPER JOBS

It is inside East India House itself that the most written-about and eccentric employees worked. In a deliberate effort to widen its intellectual base and improve the quality of its memoranda, John Company invited some legendary writers to work for it. This may be the origin of today's Foreign Office tradition of punctilious prose and intellectualism.

Thomas Love Peacock, Shelley's best friend, managed to continue penning his satirical, pomposity-puncturing novels even after rising in the company hierarchy. For 37 years, his hours were 10am to 4pm, and he was a highly valued company strategist. I have read his long, unpublished memoranda in manuscripts on subjects as diverse as steamship navigation up the Indus and the composition of Earl Grey tea. He wrote of the job: 'It is not common office routine, but very interesting and intellectual, with the possibility of being of great service to the millions of India.'

Similarly, Charles Lamb, essayist and confidant of Coleridge and Wordsworth, financed his writing life by 33 years in East India House. Although he once replied, when challenged about turning up late, 'Ah, but see how early I go!' he was a dedicated clerk. Rejoicing upon retirement on a fat pension, he soon missed the human warmth of the office, its humour and camaraderie, its 'anchoring regularity', a feeling he expressed in the anti-retirement essay 'The Superannuated Man'.

Towards the end of the EIC's life, the company employee John Stuart Mill, a brilliant philosopher, had a more baleful effect on the company, introducing the utilitarianism of his friend Jeremy Bentham into British policy towards India. Bentham's utilitarianism was a cold philosophy, an Orwellian vision reducible to this: happiness of the many is the end, even if individuality suffers. With a Stalin-like sense of his importance, Bentham directed that when he died, his body should be put on public display, fully clothed, in University College, London (it was kept like this until well into the twentieth century).

WITH A STALIN-LIKE SENSE OF HIS IMPORTANCE, BENTHAM DIRECTED THAT WHEN HE DIED, HIS BODY SHOULD BE PUT ON PUBLIC DISPLAY, FULLY CLOTHED, IN UNIVERSITY COLLEGE, LONDON.

Bentham's actions explain the philosophy better: he evicted his London tenant, Lamb's friend the essayist William Hazlitt, when Hazlitt's income dried up because of illness. As Hazlitt's biographer Duncan Wu put it, 'The bailiffs would be sent in on 25 December – a festival that, to a utilitarian, was as suitable for an eviction as any day of the year.' And Bentham destroyed poet John Milton's tree-shaded garden at 19 York Street, near St James's Park – where he had written the greatest poem in the language, *Paradise Lost* – to build a utilitarian school. Wu again: 'Hazlitt saw the destruction of the garden as symptomatic of the soullessness of the entire utilitarian project.'[1]

Imagine a utilitarian view of India, with all its mysticism, hundreds of religious holidays, unchecked population growth and untamed wildernesses. To cap it all, in India, the mentally disabled were often regarded as sacred beings. It is lucky for Bentham that he stayed in London. The reality of India might have blown his mind.

LEGACY

While John Stuart Mill agitated to change the company's old ways from within, it was battered from without by a government employee, Thomas Macaulay. He was a child prodigy, who, banging his head as a toddler, uttered these first words to his nanny: 'The pain is much abated ma'am.' The Benthamite Macaulay pressed for the closure of the Calcutta madrassa and Sanskrit College, and declared that:

'One shelf of European literature is worth more than the whole literature of India and Arabia.'

When the Government took over the administration of India from the company, all functions transferred to the current Foreign Office building. Older scholars I have known recall going to the Foreign Office to consult EIC records, some of which were found in 1973 being used to block up a draughty chimney. After 1858, a Permanent Undersecretary for India, Sir Louis Mallet, was appointed. The old ways were over: he was 'dismayed at the laxity' of company ways.

OLDER SCHOLARS I HAVE KNOWN RECALL GOING TO THE FOREIGN OFFICE TO CONSULT EIC RECORDS, SOME OF WHICH WERE FOUND IN 1973 BEING USED TO BLOCK UP A DRAUGHTY CHIMNEY.

As recent company historian Margaret Makepeace put it, 'The chain of benevolent management stretching back 250 years was broken.' Looking back mistily to Leadenhall Street, John Kaye, a contemporary of Lamb, saw 'Mr Company's venerable face, glowing with Burgundy and Benevolence'.[2]

East India House had been a seat of Empire, but it should also be remembered as a portal between two cultures, and a pioneer of the work-life balance. Modern companies, with their long and vacuous social responsibility statements, could certainly learn from 'John Company'.

Notes

1. Duncan Wu, *William Hazlitt: The First Modern Man* (Oxford University Press, 2008), pp.276.
2. Margaret Makepeace, *The East India Company's London Workers* (Boydell, 2010), p.192. Sir John Kaye, *The Administration of the East India Company* (Richard Bentley, 1853), p.623.

A WINTER'S TALE, 1598

✦ ✦ ✦

I n 1598 Shakespeare was 35 and famous enough to be attacked in print as an 'upstart crow' by a rival. Many of his plays had already been staged, including *The Merchant of Venice* and *Romeo and Juliet*. Like those later Londoners, the Rolling Stones, who set up their own record label at a similar age, he felt it was time to keep more of the profits of his labours. He had a wife and two daughters to support, rented London rooms, and had bought New Place, the largest house in Stratford-upon-Avon. He mocked the practice of buying coats of arms, but bought one himself.

SHOWBIZ PROFITS

Ironically, for the most published author in history, Shakespeare was not much interested in publication: the big money came from live performance.[1] Over 8,000 Londoners a week went to a play. So far, he had bought shares in the Chamberlain's Men, the company he acted in and wrote for, but a share in an actual theatre would really give him a piece of the action.

Enter his friend Richard Burbage, 30, a Londoner and an actor whose life was, an observer remarked, 'nothing but action'. Burbage was much loved and his death at 50 was to be widely lamented. Shakespeare was to write *Hamlet* for him, and he had played the first Romeo at a theatre owned by his father, James Burbage, in Shoreditch, north of the river. This building, the foundations of which were discovered in 2008, was called 'The Theatre' and was a magnet for Tudor playwrights. Shakespeare lived near it, and plays by Marlowe and Jonson were staged there. The odd name was partly because the idea of a purpose-built public theatre was completely novel, a Renaissance revival of that Graeco-Roman idea, the amphitheatre.

THEATRES

The theatre was a London phenomenon, not reflected in Europe, where drama was still the preserve of court masques held indoors. The complete social mixture of London's audiences has been confirmed by the recent discovery of an exquisite Italianate silver fork at Bankside's Rose Theatre site, amid remains of apple pips, nuts and oyster shells. Forks were widely regarded as laughable foreign novelties, and until well into the seventeenth century were only used by the rich.

A visiting Dutchman despaired that, having paid his penny for a performance, he was surrounded by 'a gang of porters and carters'. The audience often chatted noisily and food sellers circulated continuously among the standing 'groundlings'. We know that bottled beer was drunk, because an audience member used it when a stage effect set his breeches on fire. Drink sales could be an income stream: one of Shakespeare's actor friends ran the taphouse attached to the Rose Theatre.

THE GLOBE IS PLANNED

Burbage, Shakespeare and four other actors of their troupe contracted to build a new theatre, the Globe, in Southwark, just south of London Bridge. It would be massive, seating 3,000 (twice the current Globe capacity), but built on the cheap. The roof would be thatch, not tiles (hence it burnt down in 1613) and – the inspired idea of Burbage, who was also a trained joiner – the frame timbers would be those of his father's theatre in Shoreditch, the lease of which was about to expire. A cunning clause in the lease said that the theatre could be dismantled at any time. Although the landlord, Giles Allen, did not agree, Richard Burbage was determined to take it literally. How satisfying it would be for Shakespeare and for Burbage to relocate the theatre, which had seen the premiere of *Romeo and Juliet*.

A CUNNING CLAUSE IN THE LEASE SAID THAT THE THEATRE COULD BE DISMANTLED AT ANY TIME. ALTHOUGH THE LANDLORD, GILES ALLEN, DID NOT AGREE, RICHARD BURBAGE WAS DETERMINED TO TAKE IT LITERALLY.

For Burbage there was another emotional factor at play: his father, James, who had died recently, had fought tooth and nail to keep ownership of his Shoreditch playhouse. Charged with contempt of court in a long legal wrangle over who should get the theatre profits, James had said, 'God's blood – if there were twenty contempts I would defy them all before I would lose my possession.' When a party of men arrived with a court order demanding compliance, James said he would wipe his arse with it, and young Richard laid into the men with a broomstick.

And so Richard Burbage and his company, with a crew of carpenters and several carthorse wagons, arrived at The Theatre in Shoreditch, north of the river, to dismantle it and take its timbers nearly 3.2km (2 miles) south, over the river to a new site in Southwark, where it became the Globe. Then, as now, the journey is a 40-minute walk through the heart of London.

THEATRICAL REMOVALS

When, on that snowy morning of 29 December 1598, Burbage's men arrived, they were a formidable force. Actors possessed superior weapons and were trained to use them; the swordfights in plays were violent entertainments. The playwright Ben Jonson killed a man in a swordfight, and a spectator of *Hamlet* was to notice how, after a swordfight with Laertes, Burbage was sweating and panting.

Was Shakespeare there? Surely he would have joined in the procuring of his investment, his first theatre, when it was all happening a few hundred yards from his house? Scholars have assumed so. As we know from the subsequent court case, a crowd gathered quickly, including supporters of Giles Allen the landlord. Ellen, James Burbage's widow, was there too.

One of Allen's friends intervened and said he had power of attorney: he was ignored. As Peter Street, the master carpenter hired by Burbage, began to dismantle the theatre, a silk weaver called Henry Johnson asked him to stop. Street said he was only refurbishing the building. The day drew on. It stayed freezing cold (the Thames was 'nigh frozen' that day) and it was the Christmas season; the crowd gradually drifted home. The Brooklyn-raised Professor James Shapiro has unforgettably imagined the next stage, at about 4pm.

As darkness fell the old frame of The Theatre, loaded onto wagons, with horses slipping and straining from the burden of hauling the half-ton, foot-square oak posts, began to make its way through streets carpeted with snow.[2]

FROM SHOREDITCH TO BISHOPSGATE

The journey to the Globe's site was also a journey through the social spectrum, from low to even lower. Shoreditch, or sewer-ditch, with its boggy Walbrook river, was criticized by Puritans as full of 'disorderly, loose, insolent people living in noisome tenements'. The one old mansion was divided into insanitary bedsits for French, Italian and Spanish pieceworkers. There were beggars' shacks, gambling dens, many brothels, a ruined almshouse with old people clinging on inside, their gardens trashed by squatters, and a riotous bowling alley. It sounds rough, but it was arty bohemia compared to Southwark, to which both the theatre and Shakespeare moved in 1599.

But let us accompany the horses, steaming in the frozen night air, and the triumphant Chamberlain's Men, along the road. Leaving Shoreditch they passed straight down Bishopsgate, the old Roman

Ermine Street or Old North Road. Bishopsgate was also full of inns (just as today it is dotted with pubs and bars); the Green Dragon, the Dolphin, the Tabard, the Spread Eagle, and the Black Bull, a medieval stone house where the Black Prince once lived, have all gone. Shakespeare knew these Bishopsgate inns, although he was adroit at avoiding invitations to pub nights out, often using the excuse that he was 'in pain' (understandable, considering his workload as actor, businessman and playwright).

Here is another glimpse of Shakespeare's world and maybe of him: in about 1938 my father bought a 1599 copy of Plutarch's *Lives of the Noble Greeks and Romaines*, translated by Thomas North and published at Blackfriars. It cost a few bob in Portobello Road market. Shakespeare got many of his plots from this work, and lifted whole lines from it. The life of Coriolanus inspired Shakespeare's play *Coriolanus*, which was a direct commentary on the 1601 London rebellion of the Earl of Essex. Curiously, the book is frequently annotated in an Elizabethan hand, by someone who used it a lot, and in the margin next to Coriolanus's march into Rome is written 'Essex is going into ye citie'. Is this Shakespeare's copy? When I sent photocopies to experts I was asked to take the book to Stratford for inspection but I was too busy. (No, I was not really too busy, but I would rather live in hope, and experts are often wrong.)

CROSSING LONDON BRIDGE

The carts rumbled on downhill to the river, past Thomas More's old house, Crosby Hall, past the frozen fountain at St Helen's Church, out of Bishopsgate and on to Gracechurch Street, with its public water pump. In the daytime long queues formed at these pumps, the water source for a dense population (Tudor houses in London had an average of two lodgers). They passed into Fish Street Hill, which smelled of its market, and on to the medieval London Bridge.

This tourist wonder, London's only bridge, bore over 130 shops and buildings, some seven storeys high. Most had coal fires inside, even upstairs, which would have been crackling away cosily high above the icy waters. After years of chaos, the roadway had to be regulated: you entered London on the left, returning on the right – this is why we still drive on the left (see box). The bridge's nineteen piers were so close together that the Thames gushed in rapids between them, and the river was often 1.8m (6ft) higher upstream. 'Shooting the bridge' was an extreme sport in Tudor London.

Except in the short cul-de-sac approach road to the Savoy Hotel. This is the only road in Britain where one drives on the right. It all started because in horse-drawn carriages ladies sat behind the driver, so they could alight on the right side for the hotel entrance. The road was the scene of another traffic phenomenon: actor Steve McQueen used to arrive in his Ferrari and do a handbrake turn outside the door. I am grateful to Angus Lennie ('Ives' in *The Great Escape*), who gave me his McQueen stories when I importuned him in the Holland Park café.

On the dark river, hundreds of wherries (small water taxis) bobbed and clunked at anchor. Taxi journeys at night were mysteriously forbidden. The watermen – there were 3,000 of them in Tudor London – were a tough breed who led a tough life. Their language was notoriously foul and their wit so quick that it was said to be impossible to get the last word with them. They were like modern cabbies. The

watermen were doomed: despite their protests and petitions, the coach and sedan chair would soon all but extinguish their trade. (The big complaint about the coach, apart from it being a foreign import, was its infernal noise.) For now, they slept easy, about to experience their golden age as thousands plied their way to Bankside's sensational plays.

Dominating the bridge and straddling its roadway was the five-storey Nonsuch Palace, a marvellous wooden construction with four gilt onion domes and ornate window frames. Built in the Netherlands, it was reconstructed here and ironically named after Henry VIII's old palace in Surrey. Its ephemerality and tall, domed towers wreathed in London mist probably prompted Prospero's line about the fleeting nature of life, that 'insubstantial pageant', destined to disappear like 'the cloud-capped towers', and 'the great globe itself'. I think the towers were visible from the Globe's stage, which makes Prospero's speech a farewell elegy to Elizabethan London itself, in all its bawdy splendour, its rank magnificence. Shakespeare, the country boy who wrote the speech at the end of his playwriting career, was giving an elegiac farewell to the city.

Just before the wagons rolled off the bridge, they passed 30 heads on iron spikes (it would be only 50 years before one of them was Thomas Cromwell's). On the southern bank, a new smell hit the carthorses' nostrils as they passed through the Shambles, the butchers' quarter. Hosing down was not possible in conduit-

supplied London, as is evidenced by the complaints of players who had to act in bear-baiting arenas the day after that grisly sport has taken place.

SOUTHWARK

Nearby, Southwark Cathedral's tower loomed in the darkness, the only structure left today on Bankside from the Tudor skyline. In eight years' time, Shakespeare would attend the funeral there of his brother Edmund, and he knew Robert Harvard, a local butcher whose son was baptised there. The son, John, founded a university of some note in America.

The last few hundred yards of the journey passed several substantial inns built for travellers from the south, mostly with large courtyards surrounding stables. Just one of them remains today up a side alley, with one side of its galleried courtyard intact: the George, the only pub owned by the National Trust. Early theatre had flourished in these inns, and the name given to the ground-floor seats in a theatre – 'stalls' – is a hangover from that horsey past.

THE JOURNEY PASSED SEVERAL SUBSTANTIAL INNS BUILT FOR TRAVELLERS FROM THE SOUTH, MOSTLY WITH LARGE COURTYARDS SURROUNDING STABLES ... EARLY THEATRE HAD FLOURISHED IN THESE INNS, AND THE NAME GIVEN TO THE GROUND-FLOOR SEATS IN A THEATRE - 'STALLS' - IS A HANGOVER FROM THAT HORSEY PAST.

Beyond, in the back streets, was an almost favela-like level of poverty and open drainage. During Shakespeare's Bankside years, plague visited the area four times. Here, beyond the jurisdiction of the city fathers, lawlessness abounded. But the entertainment was great: there were several bear-baiting pits, cock-fighting and three theatres including, from 1599, Shakespeare's Globe.

Burbage, the actor and joiner, and Peter Street, the master carpenter, erected the new Globe Theatre within a few months in what is now Park Street, near the rebuilt Globe. A plaque marks the spot. The first play Shakespeare put on there was *Julius Caesar* and, with pleasurable anticipation, he must have visited the room where the takings box was counted – the 'Box Office'– and reflected on the success of Burbage's courageous scheme. Living in Southwark, newly secure, Shakespeare now entered the phase which continues to astonish – the phase that included *Hamlet*, *Othello* and *King Lear*.

TRACES OF SHAKESPEARE

It is said that madness awaits those who try to write a biography of Shakespeare, but in London you can catch glimpses of him that are more evocative than biographies. In the British Library you can stand within inches of his handwriting. Also free to visit, in the National Portrait Gallery, is a portrait painted from life. Viewing the picture is an extraordinary experience. Its provenance is traceable all the way back to John Taylor, the reputed painter who was described in 1719 as 'an intimate friend'. With his full lips, gold earring and flowing hair, Shakespeare seems about to smile.

In 1616, Shakespeare died aged 52, possibly after a drinking bout. In his will, among the family bequests, he left £26 to Richard Burbage. The Globe Theatre was demolished by Cromwell's Puritans in 1644.

Notes
1. Stephen Greenblatt, *Will in the World* (Jonathan Cape, 2004), p.330.
2. James Shapiro, *1599: A Year in the Life of William Shakespeare* (Faber, 2005), p.7.
I cannot, however, agree with Shapiro that Burbage would have taken the timbers over the river by boat to avoid bridge tolls.

THOMAS MORE: FROM CONKERS TO COMPASSION

✦ ✦ ✦

T homas More (1478–1535) has a miserable reputation because of his grim visage in pictures and austere portrayal on film. In fact, he was a magnetic, sparkling figure with a very 'London' sense of humour – quick, earthy and inventive. He was born near St Paul's Cathedral in Milk Street.[1]

More's writings give amazing detail about his life, as he constantly used stories to illustrate his points. So we know that as a boy in Milk Street he played conkers, quoits, 'fotebal' with a pig's bladder, whacked cherrystones with marrowbone bats, and made castles with tile shards. He grew up to astonish Europe with his intellect,

UTOPIA CAUSED A SENSATION AND GAVE US A NEW IDEAL, BUT IT WAS ONLY ONE OF MANY WORKS BY A MAN WHO ALSO REFORMED THE LEGAL SYSTEM, PIONEERED HUMANIST LEARNING, WROTE MYSTICAL CLASSICS AND IMPROVED LONDON BRIDGE, ON WHICH HIS HEAD WOULD BE IMPALED.

becoming a towering figure in the Renaissance. His still widely read *Utopia* caused a sensation and gave us a new ideal, but it was only one of many works by a man who also reformed the legal system, pioneered humanist learning, wrote mystical classics and improved London Bridge, on which his head would be impaled. When he was beheaded for not backing one of Henry VIII's marriages (to Anne Boleyn), the courts of Europe were outraged.

MORE'S LONDON

This great intellect was rooted in medieval London. More was born in 1478 and grew up right in its centre. His grandfather could have met Chaucer. The Milk Street area, now mostly finance houses, was a seething network of markets and traders, more like a Marrakech souk than anywhere in London today.

Superstition abounded. A bit of the True Cross was treasured at nearby St Paul's Cathedral, where once a year a buck was brought to the high altar and killed, as horns were blown throughout the city. On Midsummer's Night, London doorways were 'shadowed with green birch, long fennel, St John's wort and lilies'. Lord of Misrule ceremonies lingered: annually a 'boy bishop' processed in London and gave a 'sermon' in which he could freely insult the pomposity of adult clergy. Nobody could interrupt this child on pain of an anathema, a papal curse.

The Reformation was about to drive these old practices into the shadows, but their spirit survived in the irreverence of London humour. Those modern-day London creations, Max Miller, Tommy Cooper and Tony Hancock, perpetrated subversive tomfoolery. A Tom Fool was the character in a medieval street pageant, a jester who could 'speak truth to power'. Henry VIII still had one and so did More himself at home, one Henry Patenson. For More, it also was a way of looking after a simpleton – Henry had fallen from a steeple – in line with his lifelong charity work (so many destitute folk gathered at his house that he had a homeless shelter built in his garden).

MORE'S HUMOUR

The first record of the humorous More is from Christmas comic shows at Lambeth Palace, where, as a page boy, he would 'suddenly step in among the players' and exceed them all in japery, this at the same time as a nobleman noted his 'more than human' intelligence (see box).

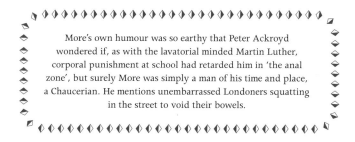

More's own humour was so earthy that Peter Ackroyd wondered if, as with the lavatorial minded Martin Luther, corporal punishment at school had retarded him in 'the anal zone', but surely More was simply a man of his time and place, a Chaucerian. He mentions unembarrassed Londoners squatting in the street to void their bowels.

As a bright young lawyer in 1499, he sat next to fellow intellectual Erasmus at a banquet, without knowing who he was. Erasmus was so impressed by his conversation that he said 'You must be More or no one', eliciting the reply 'You must be Erasmus or the devil.' The two became close and in More's city house Erasmus wrote *In Praise of Folly* and became close to More's family, his wife Alice and four children.

Erasmus wrote the best sketch of the real More: 'A complexion warm not pale, eyes greyish-blue, with a kind of fleck in them … his expression shows the sort of man he is, always friendly and cheerful, with something of the air of a man who smiles easily. He is one disposed to be merry.'

A CHELSEA IDYLL

More was careless in his dress and indifferent to fine food. This is not the boring saint of the history lessons. The inventory has survived for that City house, called 'Old Barge', near Mansion House: it included 300 books, two looms, a big world map and a large birdcage. After More became Chancellor and, as the king's chief adviser, was given his signet ring to seal royal documents, stress increased – 'the busy maze of this devil called business', as he called it.

More's solution to that stress was to move away from the city to the riverside village of Chelsea. There he had a monkey, rabbits, mulberry trees, a crab-apple orchard and a garden retreat in which he could meditate and pray. His children studied hard but he was an educational pioneer, using archery, for instance, to teach Greek letters and rearing them to make *eutrapelia*, or stimulating conversation. Radically, he thought girls and boys 'equally suited for studies'. Not until 1920 would Oxford, More's old university, admit women.

King Henry VIII came to More's house at Chelsea by royal barge and walked in the garden with his arm around More's shoulders. That evening they spent time on the roof stargazing. As historian Seymour House has said, 'his extraordinary personality' seemed to attract all who came near him. That much of this charm was his humour is evidenced by his own belief that 'If we be not merry in spirit we fail God's vision.' Seeing a courtier criticized at a court masquerade for wearing an undignified jester costume he said 'No, no. Excuse him. It hurts the state less when wise men go in fools' coats than when fools go in wise men's.' When his son congratulated him on his promotion at court he said with prophetic humour: 'If my head could win him one castle in France off it would go.'

ARREST AND TRIAL

In 1534, More was arrested for high treason after a persistent refusal to support Henry's plan to reject papal authority and make himself 'Defender of the Faith'. The king had arrived at this stance largely because of papal opposition to his marriage proposals. More knew the law so well that he had avoided entrapment for years. The sole evidence against him was one conversation with Richard Rich, Solicitor-General, and 'lesser hammer' of Henry's arch-fixer Thomas Cromwell (see box). Rich was remarkable as someone in high office who actually tortured suspects in the Tower himself, turning the wheels of the rack on many, including a woman.

After More's show trial, during which a judge called his frequent silences 'a sure demonstration of a corrupt and perverse nature', he spent a year in the Tower of London before

> Five years later Thomas Cromwell was accused of high treason and beheaded at the Tower. His last letter to Henry ended 'I cry for mercy mercy mercy.'

execution. You can stand in his unchanged first-floor cell at the Bell Tower. From there he wrote to his daughter Margaret, 'I am the King's true faithful subject and daily beadsman [one who prays for another] and pray for his Highness and the Realm. I do nobody harm, I say none harm, I think none harm and if this be not enough to keep a man alive, in faith I long not to live.'

CHANGE OF HEART

Despite all his more famous books it was *The Dialogue of Comfort Against Tribulation*,[2] written in prison, which many think his finest. Having written in Latin most of his life, this was done in English, an English as direct as anything in Tudor prose. Having read it, it contains much conventional theology but a quite out-of-its-era tolerance. It is an uncomfortable fact that More had persecuted heretics and believed in burning them. But in this book, facing death himself, he took a gentler view of human frailty, suggesting that if a fine young lady, 'good enough, left her old-acquainted knight and lay abed with a new knave', God had 'sent a storm towards her' and she merited understanding.

Take any man of great sin, he suggested, and he would grow into remorse, but guilt should have a limit, it is important that sorrow not 'swallow him up'. 'When God sends the tempest, he wants shipmen to get to their tackle and do their best so the sea does not take them over.' This is a new More. At one point of theological disputation he even says, almost to himself, 'I am not going to break my brain over this.'

'DO OLD MEN TALK TOO MUCH? YES. BUT ISN'T THAT THE JOY OF AN OLD FOOL'S LIFE, TO SIT WELL AND WARM WITH A CUP AND A ROASTED CRAB APPLE, AND DRIVEL AND DRINK AND TALK?'

More celebrated the idea of a harmless old age in terms which obviously described what would have awaited him at Chelsea: 'Do old men talk too much? Yes. But isn't that the joy of an old fool's life, to sit well and warm with a cup and a roasted crab apple, and drivel and drink and talk?' True happiness, he said in an unforgettably rich simile, 'runs about like sparkles of fire among the reeds'.

EXECUTION

On a July dawn he was taken out to be beheaded, having learned quite late that Henry had commuted his sentence of disembowelling. His immediate family were not allowed to be present, but his stepdaughter Alice was in the crowd. Someone offered him wine, which he refused. Someone else moaned about their outstanding legal case. More was a mile from Milk Street, where he had been born at 3am some 57 years earlier. His humour did not stop. Debilitated by imprisonment, he asked the jailer for help getting up the scaffold but said: 'Don't worry, I'll be all right getting down.' He cheered up the axeman by telling him not to damage his beard, tipping him a soverign and forgiving him.

Notes

1. This is my chance to recommend the begetter of this piece, Peter Ackroyd's marvellous *The Life of Thomas More* (Chatto and Windus, 1998), a rare mix of scholarship and humanity which is worthy of its subject.
2. Thomas More, *Dialogue of Comfort Against Tribulation* (first published 1534) edited by Monica Stevens (Sheed and Ward, 1951).

ENLIGHTENMENT
LONDON

THE AGE OF MAGICAL THINKING, 1650–1800

If there's somethin' strange
in your neighbourhood
Ray Parker Jr., 'Ghostbusters'

There are more things in heaven and earth Horatio,
than are dreamt of in your philosophy.
Hamlet, I. v. 167–8

If you lifted up a hatch in the floor of Charles II's wardrobe at Whitehall Palace, a flight of stairs led down to his secret alchemical laboratory. London in the age of the Enlightenment was a capital of reason and science, but also the world capital of magic and alchemy. Even more remarkably, the science grew out of the magic. The standard, over-simplified, narrative used to go like this, broadly:

MEDIEVAL LONDON = **talismans and relic worship.**

TUDOR LONDON = **witch-burning and bull-baiting.**

ENLIGHTENMENT LONDON = **the age of reason, the birth of the modern mind, concerts by Handel, Georgian Bloomsbury, science in the ascendant.**[1]

The truth, like the truth of our human lives, is that such periodicity is fallacious. The age of reason positively sparkled with magic and obscurity. Astrology, for instance, might be nonsense, but it was the begetter of both astronomy and psychology. Astrologers mapped both the stars and the unconscious. The elite of world astrology flourished in Enlightenment London, encouraged by the fame of John Dee. Dee, who partly inspired Prospero in *The Tempest*, lived at Mortlake by the Thames (today in west London) with his huge collection of books, manuscripts and automata. There he communed with spirits and cast horoscopes for the great. Queen Elizabeth set her coronation date on Dee's recommendation.

THE ASTROLOGY CRAZE

In 1672 the Recorder of London declared the practice of astrology legal, and from 1682 a Society of Astrologers met monthly in St Martin's Lane. (There was a rival 'Astrology Club' at Tower Hill, run by a Wapping tailor.) In Upper Titchfield Street, near Oxford Street, lived a carpenter's son, Ebenezer Sibly, until about 1799 (nobody is sure when he died, in obscurity). Sibly, the bestselling writer on astrology of his day, is being rediscovered as an Enlightenment radical, whose studies led him to champion complete gender equality, natural childbirth and vegetarianism.

His anatomical drawings of the female reproductive system, all done in the service of exploring the moment of nativity, were accurate and ahead of their time.

The king of astrologers, William Lilly, owned a block of houses in the Strand and saw over 2,000 clients annually. Lilly's power was extraordinary. Decorated by the King of Sweden for his accuracy, he was consulted about strategy by Charles I, then by the Puritan government, and then by Charles II. Pepys dined convivially at Lilly's house. Londoners seemed, a pamphleteer observed, to trust Lilly more than God. In 1699 the diarist John Evelyn said that Lilly had so terrified the capital about the solar eclipse that 'People durst not go out of their houses.'

IN 1699 THE DIARIST JOHN EVELYN SAID THAT LILLY HAD SO TERRIFIED THE CAPITAL ABOUT THE SOLAR ECLIPSE THAT 'PEOPLE DURST NOT GO OUT OF THEIR HOUSES.'

Increasingly, astrology hit the high street. Lacy's in Holborn, one of the many astrology shops for the well-heeled, was popular in the 1780s. In eighteenth-century Stanhope Street, near modern Kingsway, Miss Corbyn's was open for casting charts from 9am until 9pm. Handbills for Mrs Edwards, astrologer, of Covent Garden, boasted of her training in Hungary, and offered to answer 'ALL ADMISSIBLE QUESTIONS' (open 10am until 9.30pm). In 1800 alone, unbelievably, London bookshops sold 431,000 astrology almanacs, including one written by the Professor of Mathematics at Woolwich Military Academy.[2] At the time, the total population of London was about one million, and at least 25 per cent of those would not have been able to read.

THE ROYAL SOCIETY

Perhaps the greatest scientific society the world has ever seen was the Royal Society, whose members included Robert Boyle and Isaac Newton, the diminutive genius. In 2014, its website describes the Royal Society as 'a fellowship of the world's most distinguished scientists'. Founded in 1660, it was based in a building designed by Christopher Wren, up a narrow and muddy alley off Fleet Street, Crane Court. The alley remains. On meeting nights, a sulphurous lamp burned at the Fleet Street end. Members were greeted by a porter who, 'by Newton's orders' wore an impressive gown, with a staff surmounted by the Society's arms in silver.

THE ROYAL SOCIETY, NOW IN GRAND PREMISES NEAR TRAFALGAR SQUARE, HAS BEEN AT THE FOREFRONT OF SCIENCE EVER SINCE 1660, BUT IT ORIGINATED IN THE LONDON OCCULT SCENE, WHICH WAS DOMINATED BY THE GREAT PROJECT' - ALCHEMY.

Leaving their cloaks in a small ground-floor room, members ascended 'an easy staircase' to a large meeting room overlooking a small back garden. On the second floor, collections included part of a mermaid's skull. The Royal Society, now in grand premises near Trafalgar Square, has been at the forefront of science ever since 1660, but it originated in the London occult scene, which was dominated by 'the great project' – alchemy. During the Enlightenment, more books were published in London on alchemy than in any era before or since.

ALCHEMY

What was alchemy? It was the search for two things: the philosopher's stone, which could turn base metals into silver, and the panacea, which could give eternal life. Carl Jung, towards the end of his career, came to see alchemy as mankind's collective unconscious struggle to reconcile our baser desires and our higher potential. Friedrich Nietszche was psychologically an alchemist and, according to philosopher Lesley Chamberlain, without him there could be no Freud.

Alchemy, an apparently ridiculous discipline, reaches far back into Arab, Egyptian and Indian history. In 1329 the Pope banned it and soon afterwards Henry IV outlawed it in England, but in 1689 Parliament took the time and trouble to pass a law legalizing alchemy. Newton's friend Robert Boyle, the Irish philosopher, pioneer chemist, inventor and father of Boyle's Law, had testified to Parliament that he had witnessed alchemical 'transmutation'. Boyle's 'Invisible College' of seekers included alchemists, and was the precursor of the Royal Society.

Boyle, whom Professor Michael Hunter of Birkbeck College has called 'the icon of modern science' lived for years with his sister, Lady Ranelagh, at her house in Pall Mall near today's Buckingham Palace. They were incredibly close (to an eyebrow-raising degree at the time) and she gave him companionship without the distractions of marriage. In the back garden overlooking St James's Park, he pursued scientific and alchemical interests in a purpose-built laboratory. However, when Boyle read a paper at Crane Court on alchemy, Newton rebuked him for 'going public' (whilst admitting his own life-long interest). Newton himself wrote more on alchemy than physics, and read more than anyone in history on alchemy. In 1693 he wrote of drawing close to the heart of 'the process'[3] but then entered a deep depressive illness, possibly suffering from mercury poisoning.

SIGISMUND BACSTROM

One of the most endearing London alchemists was a Prussian ship's surgeon, Sigismund Bacstrom (well, he sounds Prussian but nobody knows where he came from). Permanently impoverished and a keen botanist, he got himself on to several hazardous overseas scientific expeditions before finding a patron and settling down in London. Edward Shute, 'a lover of Chymical Experiments', set him up with a laboratory in Paradise Row, Marylebone. Bacstrom joined the Rosicrucians, a Dan Brown-style secret society, allegedly ancient but in fact founded in 1740 by a French count to further alchemy. After Shute died, Bacstrom went off on expeditions again but, disgusted by the mistreatment of native tribes in North America, he settled again in London in 1804. His new patron, a Scottish printer called Alexander Tilloch, joined the Rosicrucians and set Bacstrom up in a laboratory in the East End – Albion Street, just south of Commercial Road.

The Prussian was unhappy with Tilloch's Scottish frugality, complaining of the 'excessively dirty' hut he had to live in, 'inaccessible without boots'. But the secret work proceeded. Often, all windows had to be thrown open as 'poisonous vapours' threatened suffocation. Surprisingly, Bacstrom was not alone, and conversed with at least five other working alchemists in the East End. Ever hopeful, he visited an old man in Hackney whose father had apparently, after spending £40,000 on the 'Great Secret', made gold. In Chelsea, Frederic Lafontaine showed Bacstrom his 'lead-based' alchemy, whilst a Dutch widow and suspected witch in Finsbury Square, Mrs Van Hest, also proved worth interviewing. Bacstrom, who once sold his clothes to buy apparatus, embodies the spirit of enquiry of Enlightenment London, despite the eccentricity of his goal.

PETER WOULFE

A truly eminent scientist who was mad for alchemy was Peter Woulfe, 'the last alchemist', a multilingual genius who made important discoveries about acids, distillation and mineralogy. Elected a fellow of the Royal Society in 1767, his first laboratory was a room at Clerkenwell, donated by the Earl of Bute, but he soon moved to his long-term home on the second floor in

Barnard's Inn, a secluded Inn of Court off Holborn (much of it still exists). Here he would die, sitting up alone, with a serene expression, in 1803. The Victorian antiquary John Timbs met the aged treasurer of the Inn and recorded irresistible memories of him in *Curiosities of London* (1855):

> *His chambers were so filled with furnaces and apparatus, that it was difficult to reach the fireside. I once put down my hat, and could never find it again, such was the confusion of boxes, packages, and parcels, around the room. His breakfast hour was four in the morning; a few friends were occasionally invited, and gained entrance by a secret knock.*

Woulfe attributed his failure as an alchemist to his lack of piety. As a chemist, today he might be a Nobel laureate.

THE CABALA CLUB

Alchemical London has been neglected by science historians partly because alchemy was a secret art, vulnerable to ridicule. Timbs noted that, as late as 1850, the female author of a two-volume alchemy book chose to remain anonymous, and that 'a man of wealth and position in the metropolis' was being blackmailed for 'considerable sums of money' because of his alchemy experiments.

Although no alchemist, even Sir Christopher Wren, the great mathematician-architect of St Paul's Cathedral, was inspired by magical traditions. Wren was both a Freemason and a member of the Cabala Club, which met upstairs at the Sun Tavern next to St Paul's churchyard, to discuss topics that were off-piste in Royal Society meetings. This little-known club, written about in coded shorthand by a member, John Byrom, counted among its members two presidents of the Royal Society, including Sir Hans Sloane, a great admirer of John Dee. Sloane's collections, which included over 400 books on alchemy and John Dee's 'scrying stone', a crystal of mysterious origin, became the British Museum. You can still see Dee's stone there. One typical evening, the Cabala Club discussed 'the miracles of Moses, and how modern magicians could do the like'.[4]

WILLIAM STUKELEY

Another Royal Society fellow with eccentric views was William Stukeley, a trained doctor. To free him up for arcane studies, he was given the sinecure post of vicar of St George's Church, Bloomsbury, by his patron, the Duke of Montagu, in 1747. The scholarly vicar was revered as the father of archaeology by luminaries such as Edward Gibbon (whose *Decline and Fall of the Roman Empire* was published in 1776). Stukeley's huge, 60cm-tall (2ft) volumes on Stonehenge and Avebury remain indispensable to archaeologists today.

His 41 volumes of diaries reveal that he was as occult-minded as his close friend Newton (of whom he wrote the first biography). He frequently applied to read papers

ROMANTICALLY INVOLVED WITH A MARRIED WOMAN, MIRIAM, HE APPOINTED HER A DRUIDESS, STYLED HIMSELF AN ARCH-DRUID AND EXPLORED THE ORGASM AS AN ELECTRO-MAGICAL EVENT.

on astrology to the Society, and interpreted Avebury's layout as a complex alchemical symbol. Romantically involved with a married woman, Miriam, he appointed her a Druidess, styled himself an Arch-Druid and explored the orgasm as an electro-magical event. Naturally, Stukeley was also a keen

Freemason. Some of his ideas were indeed 'far out', but they were the result of the atmosphere of free-thinking enquiry of Enlightenment London. Free of later academic limits on what constituted a proper field of study, science went far and deep.

LEGACY

The astrologers' heirs are psychologists and astronomers. The alchemists were the fathers of chemistry and quantum physics. Newton explored gravity, but he was more interested in the mysterious universal force behind it, which he called the *sal nitrum*. Boyle's work on air, vacuums and transmutation is the basis of the internal combustion engine.

London's magical thinkers remain, as historian Patrick Curry puts it, a valuable test of our ability to transcend our prejudices.

Notes
1. The two experts John Brewer (*The Pleasures of the Imagination: English Culture in the Eighteenth Century*, Routledge, 2013) and Roy Porter (*Enlightenment: Britain and the Making of the Modern World*, Allen Lane, 2000) both ignore the occult life of Enlightenment London.
2. Paul Kléber Monod, *Solomon's Secret Arts: The Occult in the Age of Enlightenment* (Yale University Press, 2013), p.235. Monod inspired much of this essay, and must be applauded for his Falstaffian author photo.
3. B. J. Dobbs, *The Janus Faces of Genius: The Role of Alchemy in Newton's Thought* (Cambridge University Press, 1991) pp.293–305.
4. Monod, p.214.

DOWNSTAIRS
IN PICCADILLY

✦ ✦ ✦

D ownstairs and behind an innocuous doorway in Piccadilly, there is a bank-vault door behind which is the cause of an act of war by Sweden in 1783. This is the only time Sweden has taken up arms against Britain. What could have so incensed the peaceable Swedes?

The story begins in a peasant's hut in southern Sweden in 1707. There the parents of Carl Linnaeus found that their toddler was always calmed when he was given a flower. They gave him his own little garden and, although his school said he was a loser, he went on to found the system of species classification that is still used today. Most of the plants we know were first described by Linnaeus. Linnaeus's home in Uppsala is a museum now, a near-sacred place to Swedes.

Linnaeus visited London once and spent time at the Chelsea Physic Garden, the magical walled garden of the Society of Apothecaries, which only opened to the public in 1983. Although the curmudgeonly Scottish head gardener resisted the new classification system, Linnaeus was revered by most of the greats of the Enlightenment: Rousseau, Goethe, and British Museum founder Hans Sloane, whose collections Linnaeus looked at while in London.

THE NATURAL HISTORY COLLECTION OF LINNAEUS

Despite this distinguished career, ending as rector at Uppsala University, Linnaeus had no family pot of money, unlike so many aristocratic scientists of the day. He fathered seven children (one died after fifteen days) and, soon after his death, his widow Sara was struggling to support the family. Sara had one massive asset, Carl's enormous insect collection and herbarium: pressed plants which were the 'type' specimens of thousands of species. Sir Joseph Banks (Captain Cook's botanist) offered to buy the collections, but Carl's son would not allow this.

Years passed and Carl's son (also Carl) died aged 42 of jaundice, in London in 1783. Sara knew what to do with the collections, now damaged by mice and moths. She contacted Banks. He was no longer able to buy the material but he had a friend … And so, bizarrely, a medical student and keen amateur botanist called James Smith purchased the most important natural history collection in history apart from Darwin's: 140,000 plants, 3,000 insects, 3,000 letters and 1,600 books. He paid the knock-down price of 900 guineas.

JAMES SMITH PURCHASED THE MOST IMPORTANT NATURAL HISTORY COLLECTION IN HISTORY APART FROM DARWIN'S: 140,000 PLANTS, 3,000 INSECTS, 3,000 LETTERS AND 1,600 BOOKS. HE PAID THE KNOCK-DOWN PRICE OF 900 GUINEAS.

King Gustav III of Sweden, a highly cultured monarch, patron and playwright, found out too late about this sad exportation and sent a man-o'-war after Smith's vessel to get Linnaeus's collection back. The expedition failed because the Swedes were insufficiently armed.

THE LINNAEAN SOCIETY

Smith established a Linnaean Society in London, with himself as the first president, and this society is still the Vatican of species classification, despite its humble doorway in Piccadilly. Here Darwin nervously presented the first draft of his theory of evolution. And here, downstairs for greater safety and ease of environmental control, is the Linnaean collection, one of London's unknown treasures. You can see it 'upon application to the secretary in writing'. The secretary has a flat above the society. The current president, Vaughan Southgate, is an eminent parasitologist who is so posh he has an entry in *Debrett's Peerage*, in thought-provoking contrast to the Swedish peasant boy who started it all.

THE MELANCHOLY KING OF KENSINGTON PALACE

✦ ✦ ✦

Britain's King William of Orange (1650–1702) had every reason to be touched by sadness. An exile – he was Dutch by birth – his mother was the daughter of the executed Charles I, and his father died before he was born. The British have always been tough on him because he was foreign. Even his title aroused mirth and one correspondent wrote, 'Can I be a lemon?'(Orange was a 14.5km/9-mile stretch of Provence, but its ancient princedom gave William a historic cachet, a Holy Roman Empire kudos.) Curiously, his subjects also grew resentful of his lack of ostentation. Wasn't he proud to be king?

He deserted Whitehall Palace (the Buckingham Palace of its day) and lived in a quiet country manor house, Kensington Palace, converted by Christopher Wren. His subjects wanted him to be a little more extrovert and glamorous, and knew little of the extraordinary battlefield courage which he showed in his youth. Rather like his ancestor, William the Silent, he could not self-advertise. His appearance did not help: with his blackened teeth and hooked nose, this short, wheezing asthmatic did not excite his 15-year-old English bride, Mary, who wept for two days at the prospect of marrying him and, privately, called him Caliban.

MARRIAGE AND MISTRESSES

William and Mary actually grew to love each other deeply and William became affectionate about her addiction to card games and gardening, and her appalling spelling. He genuinely regretted their ill-luck in having no children; Mary endured a series of miscarriages. This unlikely couple were responsible, at Kensington Palace, for one of London's cosiest gardens. Today, it is largely unchanged, and you can picture them strolling there – the king, 1.6m (5ft 6in) tall, talking up at the queen, 1.8m (5ft 11in) tall.

Prophetically, Mary, at 15, wrote that 'After too or 3 years men weary of their wives and look for mistresses.' The king's hottest affections were for his long-term mistress, the sparkling Elizabeth Villiers. Jonathan Swift called her 'the wisest woman I ever saw', and she had a huge political influence on William, but the Archbishop of Canterbury eventually persuaded the monarch to stop this liaison.

Even his two close male friends attracted a bad press and accusations of homosexuality. It is true that William's bedroom connected directly to his chums', and the royal bedroom ceiling at Hampton Court was decorated with a shepherd embracing Morpheus, the male god of sleep. William contained, like most of us, bisexual possibilities. Queen Mary herself had a long-term erotic correspondence with a woman, Frances Ashley, whom she called her 'husband'.

So you get the picture: William, naturally taciturn, foreign, a dwarfish suspected sodomite and adulterer. It was inevitable that, as a foreigner and an introvert, he would not able to win over the British public. When I worked with below-stairs staff at the palace in 1974, the poor reputation of King Billy still survived in handed-down oral tradition. And he fails the popularity litmus test – there are hardly any pubs named after him.

DUTCH HERO

William missed his youth in the Netherlands. He was born and raised in the Binnenhof Palace, an ancient warren of rooms dating back to before 1200. (It has been repeatedly slated for demolition but the Dutch people always insist on its survival. It sort of represents the stubborn, mysterious individuality of the Dutch persona, which is why even now the Dutch prime minister has his office jammed into a small tower of the Binnenhof.) There, a dashing cavalry officer, Prince Frederick of Nassau, was William's guardian and father figure, teaching the boy riding, hunting, dancing and fun. And in the Netherlands he had become a much-loved national hero, scorning French armies and Catholic alliances to protect Dutch freedom.

A conversation with Christopher Wren led to the most extraordinary expression of this Wordsworthian nostalgia. The weather vane on Wren's cupola at Kensington Palace was linked by a series of rods to a large golden compass needle on a painted map of Europe over the fireplace in the King's Chamber. William could thus see when the wind stood fair for a trip home to the Netherlands, land of his youth and popularity. The mechanism still works.

THE INCOGNITO
TSAR, 1698

✦ ✦ ✦

Tsar Peter the Great was an almost mythological figure and so his visit to London in January 1698 set the capital twittering with excitement. Only a hundred years before, a Tudor explorer described 'the Russies' as 'passing rude and addicted to vices vile'. Learning in Russia was apparently 'feared as a Monster, avoided like a Wildfire Ship'. The British invitation letter from 1698 was fairy-tale stuff:

> *Most Serene Potentate, Czar of Muscovy and Defender of the Christian Faith, who has pursued his noble intent toward our general enemy, the Turk and the Crimean Khan …*

London was in for a shock. Tsar Peter was charming and modest, and determined to use his visit to further his grand project: dragging Russia out of the Middle Ages. The 25-year-old was 2m (6ft 8in) tall, with thick brown hair and long-lashed black eyes, and had survived a dangerous childhood. From the age of 10 he had ruled with Sophia, his half-sister, as regent. While he sat on a huge throne, she sat behind it, quietly giving him instructions though a hole in the back. He took solace from palace politics by playing with his toy army and navy for hours. Now the British navy was his ideal. Travelling across the wintry North Sea on HMS *Yorke*, he had astonished the crew by going aloft to inspect the rigging, and he asked Admiral Mitchell, who delivered him to Strand quay by royal barge, to be his escort for his whole stay. The two men conversed fluently in Dutch.

THE CURIOUS EXPLORER

The tsar, who admired anyone who could make something, had just visited Holland, where he stayed with a blacksmith in his tiny house (now a museum). Even in Russia, Peter favoured stays in a log cabin that his soldiers had built in three days. In London he asked for humble lodgings, and stayed at 21 Norfolk Street, between the Strand and the Thames. The house opened on to the street.

From here he went on incognito journeys in London, often on foot in the snowy streets, for this was such a cold January that the Thames had frozen and people were able to walk across it; 'frost fairs' were also held on the ice. Picture a much wider Thames,

with marshy, reedy banks, for there was no Embankment until Victorian times. In 1698 the city numbered about 700,000 people.

Entering a clockmaker's to buy a watch, he stayed to learn how to take it apart and reassemble it. He visited the docks, where the forest of masts was one of the wonders of the world; Daniel Defoe once counted an unbelievable 2,000 ships. At Deptford shipyard, he studied shipbuilding by actually joining the carpenters at work. He visited Parliament, but was apparently spotted, in a 'green vest trimmed with furr'. His one attempt at theatre-going ended early as he was identified, with his outlandishly dressed friends, in the interval.

Visiting Greenwich, he talked mathematics at length with the Astronomer Royal, Edmond 'Comet' Halley, and hired a mathematics professor to found a maths academy in St Petersburg. The tsar was similarly impressed by Christopher Wren's St Paul's Cathedral, parts of which were newly opened. At the Tower of London, a canny official hid the axe that beheaded Charles I, 'lest His Majesty throw it in the Thames'. Peter's father had expressed his outrage at the regicide by expelling British merchants.

KING MEETS TSAR

King William III, respecting the tsar's desire not to be mobbed, took an unmarked coach to Norfolk Street, where he found the Emperor of All the Russias sharing a room with four other Russians. The king, struggling in the warmth with his asthma, opened a window and the two soon found they had much in common. Both spoke Dutch and shared an antipathy towards King Louis XIV of France, the Sun King, and an aversion to the trappings of royalty.

Peter returned the visit, and was impressed by the humility of William's domestic-styled red-brick Kensington Palace. He observed a ball through a small internal window, and stayed several nights. A later resident, Princess Diana, might have envied such an achievement of anonymity.

SPIRITS AND SPIRITUALITY

One evangelical observer, Bishop Burnet, recorded a man keen to educate his people, but one who 'seems designed by nature rather to be a ship-carpenter than a prince ... a man of very hot temper, he raises his natural heat by drinking too much brandy ... he is subject to convulsive motions all over his body, and his head seems to be affected with these'. Burnet was peeved that he failed to convert Peter to Anglicanism, and his sneering remarks describe the petit mal epilepsy that often tugged the tsar's face to the right. Other diarists were too polite to mention this tic.

Tsar Peter was impressed by a Quaker service in London and was to sit in silence at many Quaker services in subsequent years, in Russia and Germany. He mused that 'Whoever could live by such a system would be happy.'

Away from clerics and courtiers, Tsar Peter found an unexpected soulmate in Peregrine Osborne. This master shipwright, instructed by the king to make the tsar a state-of-the-art ship, was, to Peter's astonishment, a young, hard-drinking nobleman. In a biographer's words, Osborne was 'a superb seaman, an original designer and a majestic drinker', who taught the tsar the delights of cups of brandy laced with pepper. The two frequented a pub near the Tower so often that it was renamed 'The Czar of Muscovy'. And Peter so enjoyed the company of Osborne's sexy actress friend Laetitia Cross that she moved in with him at Norfolk Street.

All this carousing was testing the tsar's anonymity. With crowds gathering in Norfolk Street, Peter moved out to Sayes Court, a Deptford manor house near the docks and owned, fortunately for us, by the diarist John Evelyn. Evelyn may be the unluckiest landlord in London history. The tenant who moved out to accommodate the tsar was Admiral Benbow.

ADMIRAL JOHN BENBOW

Benbow was a naval hero but also a popular byword for brutality and explosiveness, a veritable Lord Flashheart (the Blackadder character played by Rik Mayall).

During Benbow's career he apologised for accusatory language to a court-martial, shelled a ship with 900 bombs in one afternoon, carried on fighting after a shell smashed his leg, set St Malo ablaze, ran his own pirate-busting merchant ship, 'the *Benbow*', chased some West Indian pirates as far as Newfoundland, caused the execution of several captains who would not obey his orders, and, when attacked off Morocco, cut off and salted the heads of thirteen Moors, encasing one, if Dickens is to be believed, in silver. It is still uncertain how many children Benbow sired, and by whom.

Poor Evelyn might have been wary of letting his property to this gentleman, and after six months the diarist wrote: 'I have let my house to Captain Benbow, and have the mortification of seeing every day much of my former labours impairing for want of a more polite tenant.' But at least Benbow had paintings and chairs.

TRASHED!

The tsar and his friends wrought havoc at Sayes Court. After three months, Evelyn's friend Christopher Wren surveyed the house and pronounced it 'entirely ruined'. The carpets and even the floors had to be replaced, 50 fine chairs had been used for firewood, paintwork was battered, and bedding seemed to have been ripped by wild beasts. Over twenty paintings were ruined, some having been used as target practice. Evelyn was a famous gardener, but his lawns and bowling green were churned

> AFTER THREE MONTHS, EVELYN'S FRIEND CHRISTOPHER WREN SURVEYED THE HOUSE AND PRONOUNCED IT 'ENTIRELY RUINED'.

into mud, and his hedge, 122m (400ft) long and 2.7m (9ft) high, was wrecked. The Russians had staged drunken wheelbarrow races through it. The government paid for all the damage, including a payment to lucky Benbow for property he had lost.

PASSAGE TO THE PAST

Despite the destruction in Deptford, it was a constructive visit; the tsar went home inspired and informed, taking with him scores of English craftsmen, sailors, and even two barbers.

You can experience a sort of timeslip to the visit if you stand in the Long Gallery at Kensington Palace today. The Godfrey Kneller painting of Peter has hung in the room where it was painted ever since his visit. It is generally regarded as the best likeness of the Emperor of All the Russias in the happiness of his mid-life. He was to die at 52. Despite fathering fourteen children, no male heir survived, and so his wife Catherine, an ex-servant girl, became Russia's first woman ruler.

MOMENTS OF BEING

✦ ✦ ✦

ondon is like Tibet because it specializes in moments
of profound well-being. How strange that this noisy
city, through the ages, has sent us messages from the still
centre in all of us, like coded beeping from a distant planet
(see box).

> These moments of well-being cannot be claimed by religion,
> explained by science, or expressed in words. Rowan Williams
> cleverly hints at them by talking, appropriately in a way
> nobody can understand, of a 'sense of immanence'. The
> Dead Sea scrolls, found in 1945, still puzzle theologians with
> their insistence on 'having faith in the unseen'. Whether it's
> Hawking's parallel universe or Jung's collective unconscious,
> London is a portal to something rich and strange.

GEOFFREY CHAUCER

As early as 1387, Chaucer described an atmosphere of rebirth
so poetically that it must have been personal. He opened *The
Canterbury Tales* with what is still the best snapshot of spring in
London: a west wind blows away city smells, flowers bloom on
wasteland and 'the trees themselves are bathed in song'. Then,

he says, minds turn to thoughts of holy shrines, of pilgrimage, of a spiritual renewal to parallel that London spring.

WILLIAM SHAKESPEARE AND WALTER RALEIGH

Half a mile from Chaucer's house, 200 years later, a lodger living upstairs in Silver Street started a series of sonnets – Shakespeare's sequence, celebrating love and nature in pellucid lines, came out of a muddy Blackfriars which resembled a modern Calcutta backstreet (see box). Sonnet 30, mentioning his 'sweet sessions of silent thought', reminds us that the hurly-burly was no barrier to inner peace.

> As late as 1715, the architect Nicholas Hawksmoor saw 'no City, nor streets, but a chaos of dirty rotten sheds always tumbling and catching fire, with winding crooked passages, lakes of mud and streams of stinking mire running through them'.

A mile downriver, the Elizabethan explorer and poet Walter Raleigh kept a room in his riverside house for silent sessions of solitary meditation. The room was his favourite place in the world – and he had seen a lot of the world. In 1974, I picked up a slab on the Thames foreshore near the Strand. Turning it over, I saw a gleaming polychrome Delft image of a stag. I cycled to the Victoria and Albert Museum, where it was identified as a floor tile from one of the Tudor riverside mansions.

GEORGE FRIDERIC HANDEL

Up the hill from the Thames and just before Oxford Street, on 14 November 1741 a portly man in the upstairs bedroom of a small house wrote 'For God Alone' on the last page of an oratorio: Handel had completed *The Messiah* in 24 days, with hardly a correction. A persistent story says that he 'saw all heaven before him' as he wrote the 'Hallelujah Chorus'. The house is a museum now, so you can stand in the bedroom. The museum's office was once Jimi Hendrix's flat, where he too composed and, hearing about his predecessor, bought and played an LP of *The Messiah*.

WILLIAM BUTLER YEATS

Back by the river, in the Strand, the Irish mystical poet W. B. Yeats's most famous poem was inspired in 1888, not by the country, but by a moment standing in the Strand in spring. The opening of 'The Lake Isle of Innisfree' has become a Western mantra:

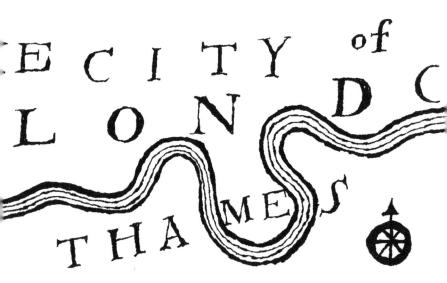

I will arise and go now, and go to Innisfree,
And a small cabin build there, of clay and wattles made.

Yeats saw a tacky window advertising a cool drink, with a
tinkling water feature, and this evoked the idea of a peace we can
always access, anywhere. That peace, the poem says, even exists
as he stands on 'the pavement grey'. Even there, 'I hear it in the
deep heart's core.'

JOHN KEATS

Four miles north in Hampstead, Keats had a similar inner
experience when, sitting in his garden under a plum tree at
eventide with 'quiet breath', he heard a nightingale. Although
Hampstead was still a country village, the 1819 'Ode to a
Nightingale' was shot through with a sadness about the
encroachment of London, 'where men sit and groan', and about
the speculative building of two large houses opposite the poet's
cottage. Like Yeats's poem, the Ode, with its 'magic casements
opening on the foam, of perilous seas in faery lands forlorn', is
an evocation of our inner wilderness, an Arcadian landscape
so besieged that Keats had often 'been half in love with easeful
death'. Bizarrely, the very threat of London drew two great
mystical nature poems out of Keats and Yeats.

WILLIAM WORDSWORTH

Only a few hundred yards from Yeats's Innisfree moment in the
Strand, Wordsworth was touched by nature in London, as he
stood on Westminster Bridge early on a summer morning in 1802.

The City now doth, like a garment, wear
The beauty of the morning; silent, bare
Ships, towers, domes, theatres, and temples lie
All bright and glittering in the smokeless air.
Ne'er saw I, never felt, a calm so deep!
The river glideth at his own sweet will
Dear God! The very houses seem asleep;
And all that mighty heart is lying still!

Amusingly, the poet received many complaints about the
illogicality of this famous poem: sleeping houses, a city both
bare and clothed, and so on – but its craziness stems straight
from the mystery of his feelings on that bridge.

GEORGE GORDON BYRON

Although the Romantic poets' longing for the visionary clarity
of childhood is associated with the Lake District, a short trip up
the Metropolitan Line takes you to a place as charged with poetic
voltage as Helvellyn. You can sit at the spot, in Harrow-on-the-Hill
churchyard, where Lord Byron sat one windy day in 1807 and
penned his 'Lines Written Beneath an Elm in the Churchyard of
Harrow'. The poem recalls his childhood reveries there.

Thou drooping Elm! beneath whose boughs I lay
And frequent mused the twilight hours away ...

Like Keats, the loss of innocence makes him muse darkly, 'With
this fond dream, methinks, 'twere sweet to die'. The spot is all
the more charged because the elm blew down in 1935, and
because Byron's daughter Allegra is buried a few feet away.
Byron's romantic death, at 36, fighting for the youth of the

Greek nation, gave him eternal cult status. When I was at his publisher's office in Mayfair one day in 1997, a beautiful girl ran in off the street, headed straight upstairs to the Byron bust on the landing, kissed it and ran out. John Murray, the descendant of the John Murray who published Byron, was with me and simply said: 'It happens all the time; we don't bother to stop them.'

ARTHUR ELPHINSTONE, SIXTH LORD BALMERINO

Lord Balmerino, an unknown figure, had a similarly Byronic moment of temporal awareness, but he had no time to write about it. Balmerino was a Scottish rebel leader beheaded at the Tower of London in 1746, after the English had crushed the rebellion and passed a law forbidding the wearing of the kilt. On his way to the Tower, near modern-day Trafalgar Square, he saw a gooseberry-seller and persuaded the redcoats to stop his cart. He ate a few gooseberries and seemed to be appreciating the sunny morning, before rumbling on his way (see box).

CHARLES LAMB

Back on the riverside, that Dickensian figure, Charles Lamb, found a profound sense of well-being (PSWB). Never rich, he lived with his sister, keeping her from the madhouse to which

Snatched food undoubtedly tastes extra good. William Carlos Williams's poem, 'This is Just to Say', is about illicitly eating plums meant for breakfast: 'Forgive me, they were delicious.'

she would have been consigned after she murdered their
father. But, up four flights of stairs in his flat in King's Bench
Walk in that leafy pedestrianized area of law firms called The
Temple, Lamb revelled in 'all the privacy of a house without the
encumbrance', able to 'lock my friends out and converse with
my immortal mind'. There, 'up and airy' as he sat in bed with a
view of the Thames and the distant Surrey hills, he found a peace
'better than any Mahomedan Paradise'.

Imagine Lamb, with his old-fashioned, Quakerish clothes,
famously hesitant speech (reminiscent of early Anthony Hopkins),
and odd, flat-footed gait. Picture a large head on small legs, a
much-lined face with 'quick-turning brown eyes' and you can
almost hear the quaint 'How d'ye do' he was known for and see
that 'sweetest smile that ever brightened a manly face'. Walking
in London he confessed that he

> often shed tears in the motley Strand from fullness of joy at so
> much life ... watchmen, women of the town, waggons, tradesmen,
> playhouses, the very dirt and mud, the sun shining on houses
> and pavements, old bookstalls, coffee houses, steam of soup from
> kitchens, the whole pantomime of London. These things feed me.

Lamb – whose children's version of Shakespeare still sells steadily
– had something of the mystic about him. Even decades after his
death, his friend Thackeray, finding one of Lamb's letters, put it
to his forehead and whispered, 'Saint Charles'.

G. K. CHESTERTON

In 2013 the canonization was proposed of an even more
unlikely figure – the portly, Falstaffian thinker and novelist G.

K. Chesterton. Like Lamb, 'G. K.' was far too interesting to be a saint, and his London PSWB moment happened in 1932. He 'had a vision between two cups of coffee in a Gallic café in Soho'. Hard to summarize, he had a sudden awareness, in common with many who have narrated their near-death experiences, of the connectedness of all the millions around him and knew, too, a cheap music-hall song to be as good as any aria.

VIRGINIA WOOLF

Virginia Woolf's struggle to escape 'the ghetto of language' drove her mad in the end, but not before she had come as close as any Londoner to expressing what she called 'moments of being', in novels and diaries. Although her regular childhood walks in Kensington Gardens were annoyingly 'dominated by non-being', she did once stop and truly see a puddle. It seemed so vividly real that time stopped and 'experience avalanched'.

Another such moment, on a walk in 1925 around Tavistock Square near the British Museum, was 'a great, involuntary rush', an overwhelming sense of how we are like 'fishes in a stream', static but in a flow of time. That experience spawned her modernist masterpiece *To The Lighthouse*.

EDWARD THOMAS

I have told how mud and spring, chaos and cafés have turned
Londoners into Gnostics. Two world wars inspired further
'gnostikoi', to use Plato's word for those who gain knowledge
beyond words. After much prevarication, First World War poet
Edward Thomas had enlisted in 1915 and was about to join his
unit when, in Brunswick Square, a wave of emotion enveloped
him. As he watched some children play under sunlit plane trees
he knew that his only 'guiding drive' was the modest pleasure
of such a moment, not patriotism, and not even love. In France,
having survived the terrible Battle of Arras in 1917, he was
tragically killed by a concussion wave from a stray shell while
standing and quietly lighting his pipe.

HAROLD NICOLSON

In the Second World War the diplomat Harold Nicolson was on
fire-watching duty at the Houses of Parliament. On a night of
heavy bombing, he entered the empty chamber, and sat in the
Speaker's chair. The only lighting was his torch and, with bombs
crashing around him, he knew intensely the fragility of the whole
structure of civilization (as if he had grasped impermanence, one
of Buddhism's four noble truths). More exultantly, after the tide
had turned, on the day of the victory at El Alamein, Churchill
invited Nicolson to 10 Downing Street. Dressed in his navy blue
fire warden's romper suit, Nicolson recorded, Churchill 'half-bows
and smiles "Good morning, Harold", with the emphasis on the
first syllable of "morning" '. In the basement, the two men feasted
like naughty schoolboys on sea kale, jugged hare and cherry tart.
Winston kept on muttering, 'All written in his own hand', about a
congratulatory letter from the king. Then his youngest daughter

burst in wearing an ATS uniform, silently flung her arms around his neck and hugged him. All speaking stopped. (Why is this so moving?)

THE SOUNDS OF LONDON

A few days later, in silence, waiting on the platform of a bomb-damaged London station that post-Blitz spring, Noël Coward was suddenly 'overwhelmed by a wave of emotion'. Londoners had survived so much, supporting each other through it all. On the spot, Coward began to write the song 'London Pride', an anthem based on the old street-seller's cry: 'Won't you buy my sweet-smelling lavender?' (see box).

Other composers sampled London's soundscape: Vaughan Williams put the Westminster Abbey bells in his *London Symphony*, and John Ireland's *London Overture* centres on the cry of the Number 9 bus conductor: 'Dilly, Picca-dilly'. Another fruitful bus was the Number 11: Laurie Lee once wrote an entire poem sitting on the top deck.

The little saxifrage called London Pride thrives in dry, stony habitats including bomb sites.

JACQUETTA HAWKES

An arresting soundscape, including silence, often triggers these moments of awareness in London's inner history, from Chaucer's birdsong onwards. A 41-year-old archaeologist of Minoan civilization, Jacquetta Hawkes, experienced a gnosis in 1951 in her back garden in Primrose Hill. One starlit night, lying on her back in the grass, she heard a barge hoot on the Regent's Park canal. Then a steam train whistled from Euston, and silence returned. She became 'suddenly conscious of the huge city spreading for miles on all sides, of innumerable fellow creatures stretched horizontally in beds, of a bargee leaning sleepily on his long tiller, of people in lighted train carriages, of the earth, of her cat jumping down nearby'. This moment begins her unclassifiable book of 'dream-time geology', *A Land*, reprinted after a long oblivion in 2013, with a quiet green cloth cover (see box).

I had an experience 38 years ago which I can neither classify nor forget, one which I return to in my mind frequently, but have never written down or told to anybody for fear of losing it in words. Edward Thomas once called his experience 'something secret and sealed, almost pagan'. After heavy rain, in a Chelsea square near Bram Stoker's house, the afternoon sun came out and gilded the tall, wet plane trees. Then a sudden strong gust shed sheets of golden drops on to wet gravel and I felt shocked at how the world can suddenly, almost ridiculously, become magical. I felt moved beyond words, as if by some hidden force.

CARVING SILENCE, 1670

+ + +

David Esterley is a tall, septuagenarian Californian with floppy white hair. His Cambridge Ph.D. was on Yeats, but he is a woodcarver. At a party, when answering a woman's 'What do you do?' question, he noticed

> *a look I'd seen before, a sudden brightening of curiosity, tinged with scepticism. She wasn't sure what to ask next, but she wanted to ask something. The creature in front of her had wandered in from some distant place. An ambergris collector. A pearl diver. She looked at me with an expression I can't describe, but it was something like nostalgia.*

DISCOVERING GRINLING GIBBONS

Back in the 1980s, Esterley was walking down Piccadilly with his girlfriend Marietta when she stopped outside St James's Church and said 'Let's go see Grinling Gibbons!' Although they were late to meet his parents for the first time, he went in. (So many great

moments happen in that delicious Narnia-land where we are late.)
The historian Jenny Uglow changes her itineraries in the West
End to incorporate a walk through the church to see Gibbons's
work. I rested in there once before a disciplinary meeting devised
to try and sack me, and Gibbons pretty much made me think: 'To
hell with them; *Ars longa, vita brevis*' (see box).

Inside the church, chillin'
angels lounge over
the organ twiddling
their trumpets, waiting
deliciously for a
better London, a new
Jerusalem. The fact that
Blake was baptized there,

'Art lasts, life is short.' I survived. The
would-be sacker was sacked. I have
toned down the language of what I
thought, for the gentler reader.

and that the church does so much to care for London's homeless,
adds to its visionary atmosphere. It hosts all sorts of spiritual
traditions, and the churchyard fronting Piccadilly has both a
street market, which puts stall rental into church coffers, and
a free counselling caravan. In 2010 it hosted the festive funeral
of Soho dandy Sebastian Horsley. Here, they built a life-sized
version of Israel's border wall and invited the public to draw
graffiti on it. And here too grows, within a cupid's bowshot of
Piccadilly Circus, an Indian bean tree. Esterley recalls that first
sight of the Gibbons carvings:

> *Floating on the wall was a shadowy tangle of vegetation,*
> *carved to airy thinness. My steps slowed. I stopped and*
> *stared. It seemed one of the wonders of the world. The traffic*
> *in Piccadilly went silent. I was taking this thing in with*
> *body and mind at once. I felt a tingling in the palms of my*
> *hands. I was an observer but somehow felt I was creating*
> *the object. Yeats writes about reading the Odyssey and*
> *feeling the salt wind blowing …*

GIBBONS IN DEPTFORD

A similar feeling overcame the courtier and diarist John Evelyn in 1671 when he discovered the woodcarver Gibbons in Deptford. Today Deptford is a friendly, roistering place by the lower Thames, despite the traffic belting through it. It is worth getting off at the Docklands Light Railway station and pottering in the truly 'London' street market, where you can buy satsumas and old flares, celeriac and an alarm clock. Deptford is full of small businesses: wedding stationery, personalized chocolates, a vinyl record shop, a 1948-established radio shop. Marlowe was stabbed and killed there, and when I was in Sainsbury's a boy ran in to escape an attacker with a knife.

Back to January 1671, and a wet and stormy winter in semi-rural Deptford. John Evelyn, with his long-nosed poetic face and shoulder-length black wig, was walking in the damp fields near his house when he happened to glance in the window of a shabby, isolated cottage. Inside was a broad-shouldered man with a big, sensuous face, carving wood with a chisel. Knocking on the door, Evelyn saw carving of a delicacy and intricacy that eclipsed anything he had seen on his travels in Europe. He chatted to Gibbons, a charming young Englishman who had been brought up in Rotterdam, where his father was a draper. He spoke with a Dutch accent.

SHIPS' CARVINGS

Although Gibbons's early training in Holland is a mystery, he seems to have carved ships' figureheads at Deptford shipyard. Founded by Henry VIII, the yard covered 12 hectares (30 acres) in 1670 and had the greatest concentration of skilled carpenters the world has ever seen. Pepys visited at about this time, and in the wet dock counted 200 sailing ships being fitted out. These sailing ships, the biggest man-made objects apart from cathedrals, were built without corroding nails, to withstand extremes of weather. In mast ponds, masts matured for years like wine. Instinctive standards of craftsmanship were set by characters such as Mr Shish, the master shipwright. He died completely illiterate, but three lords

MR SHISH, THE MASTER SHIPWRIGHT. HE DIED COMPLETELY ILLITERATE, BUT THREE LORDS AND TWO ADMIRALS WERE AMONG HIS MOURNERS.

and two admirals were among his mourners. Turning carpentry into philosophy, he had made his own coffin, which he knelt in nightly to pray. The pride of the yard was the ornate, five-decked *Golden Hind*, Drake's ship, moored there as a floating museum on Queen Elizabeth's instructions.[1] When Evelyn told the king about Gibbons, His Majesty said he would visit the cottage, but Evelyn brought the carver to court.

Gibbons was revolutionary in carving lime wood, using over 100 different sorts of chisel, which he probably made himself. Although most of his work has been varnished, at St James's Church in Piccadilly you can see the original ghostly glory of the light-coloured wood, what Evelyn called the 'candour' of Gibbons's work. When Gibbons had a workshop on Ludgate Hill by St Paul's, his sign outside was a carved pot of flowers: its leaves trembled when coaches passed.

PRESTIGIOUS COMMISSIONS

Gibbons's work is a golden thread in London's interiors – from St Mary Abchurch, tucked away in Abchurch Yard off roaring

Cannon Street, to Kensington Palace; and from Hampton Court Palace to St Paul's Cathedral, where he managed to carve life-sized forget-me-nots. Sadly, we cannot see his carvings over the fireplace at the old Admiralty in Whitehall, now part of the Foreign Office. There he carved an incredible array of navigational instruments with articulated parts, including a gunner's quadrant, a sextant and a telescope. His masterpiece, the Cosimo Panel, carved for the Duke of Tuscany, is in Florence, a *trompe l'oeil* illusion of feathers, foliage and birds which has survived both flood and fire.

Success did not come immediately, however: a French maid delayed royal approval by convincing the Queen that Gibbons was rubbish. He was under-appreciated for years. His signature was five peas in a pod: it is said that he left the pod shut if he was underpaid. Gibbons's phonetic spelling did not help his career. Here is an example, which incidentally gives us a time-machine experience of Londoners' speech in 1680:

I ombly thankyou for your great faver and extrornery ponuality I got the 50 pounds which I shall allwaes aknowligs as a pertickeler faver.
Your obegent sarvant
Grinling Gibbons

Even when he at last bought a new house overlooking the fashionable Covent Garden piazza, it was purchased on the cheap and soon collapsed.

REVELATIONS AT HAMPTON COURT PALACE

A fairly recent event has given us more information about Gibbons's art. In 1986 poor old Lady Gale, 86, who lived upstairs in a grace-and-favour flat at Hampton Court, lit a candle and started a fire which killed her and caused £5 million of damage. Charred bits of Gibbons carving were swaddled in coffin-like boxes to await restoration. David Esterley was flown in from America, took a bus out there and began to restore the carvings. In doing so, he discovered more of Gibbons's genius.

The Victorian critic Ruskin had always admired the miraculous fact that Gibbons never sanded down his work. In the same way that Ben Jonson said Shakespeare never seemed to do corrections, and Salieri fumed at Mozart's one-off fluency, Gibbons got it right first time. But Esterley noticed fine striations on some surfaces. What could this be? Sandpaper was a Victorian innovation. A chance visit from a harpsichord restorer solved the mystery. The restorer knew from old texts that the striations were made by Dutch rush (*Equisetum hyemale*). 'Sounds like a drug,' said Esterley, who went on to track down the plant and use it in his restoration work. Dutch rush, or scouring rush, was also used to clean pans.

IN THE SAME WAY THAT BEN JONSON SAID SHAKESPEARE NEVER SEEMED TO DO CORRECTIONS, AND SALIERI FUMED AT MOZART'S ONE-OFF FLUENCY, GIBBONS GOT IT RIGHT FIRST TIME.

Another discovery revealed by Lady Gale's tragic death is just how hard it was for Gibbons to get enough good lime wood. One large panel was carved on the underside of an old, chisel-scarred workbench top. But what drove Esterley to quote Yeats a lot in his book, *The Lost Carving*, was Gibbons's artistry, the way he carved delicate bay leaves *behind* carvings, in places that could never be seen. Esterley went home on the bus after discovering this and, 'over a glass or two more wine than usual', with his daughter Flora on his knee, puzzled over such hidden carving with Marietta, by now his wife. She pointed out that, on cathedral walls, medieval statues have carved backs 'because God sees them'. 'That's preposterous,' he said and she replied: 'It's not preposterous, it's a metaphor.' When he said 'For what?' Marietta was silent: some things are best left unsaid.

After that came a further Gibbons revelation. He loved music, and his cartouches of scores and instruments are breathtaking. A musicologist has discovered that his carved music scores are exact, identifiable contemporary music.

In case I have made Gibbons's work sound laboured, it was praised for *sprezzatura*, a Renaissance desideratum meaning 'a certain nonchalance'. Added to that, Esterley says, when carving like Gibbons the space you make under the leaves is almost what you are carving. You are carving silence. At Hampton Court Palace the American often worked late, alone, re-carving Gibbons:

> *I prized this solitude. I was in an island of light, lapped by soft chisel sounds, in a sea of blackness and quiet. The panelling grew companionable in the stillness. When a cold wind rattled the window, I'd close and bar the great oak shutters and imagine myself in the hold of a wooden ship.*[2]

Notes

1. Edward Walford, *Old and New London* (1878), Volume 6, pp.143–64. The *Golden Hind* was built, improbably, at the coastal village of Aldeburgh in Suffolk.
2. *The Lost Carving* by David Esterley (Duckworth/ Overlook Press, 2013), pp.26, 44, 186. I have also used Esterley's exhibition catalogue, *Grinling Gibbons* (Victoria and Albert Museum, 1998).

VICTORIAN LONDON

A GHOST STORY, 1882

✦ ✦ ✦

This obscure psychic experience from the archives of the Society for Psychical Research, concerning a headmaster and a widow, is compelling for many reasons. The narrator gives all the circumstantial detail that is so often lacking, and he is clearly a 'normal' person, not predisposed to such experiences. And on top of this, although it is understated, this is clearly something of a love story.

John Hernaman, fellow of the Society of Antiquaries and headmaster of Lambeth Boys' School, was staying in Salvador House, Bishopsgate, in the City, some way north of the Tower of London. It was a grand old house, long demolished, which had once been the residence of the Spanish ambassador. Not needing the use of most of the house, Hernaman gave up three rooms for his housekeeper and her 18-year-old son to use. He occupied two very large upstairs rooms, which communicated with each other.

A PHOSPHORESCENT APPARITION

One night, from a sound sleep in that quiet house, Hernaman
suddenly found himself wide awake and there, in an alcove of
the thick old wall, stood a little woman in her nightdress and cap,
with a small black-and-white checked shawl over her shoulders.
He was struck by the beauty and transparency of her complexion,
but also by a soft light that lay on the figure, 'such as you see
on your fingers when you rub a match, or the liquid gleaming
phosphorescence you sometimes see ridging wavelets of the sea'.
An intense feeling passed up his body from his feet up to his
head, where he felt his hair literally beginning to stand on end.
Annoyed with himself for such a hallucination, he turned away
from it. And at that moment, St Botolph's Church in Bishopsgate
chimed a quarter to two in the morning.

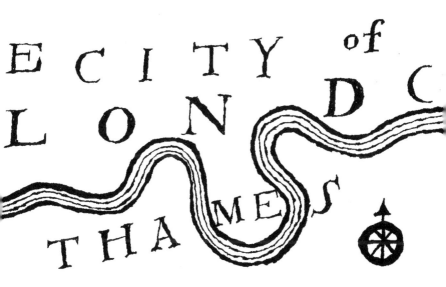

THE WIDOW

Hernaman slept undisturbed until morning, and upon going downstairs he met his best friend, Reverend George Wrench, and exclaimed, 'Laugh at me! Here am I, a man supposed to be educated, of average intelligence, living in the very centre of civilization, an utter disbeliever in ghosts, yet last night I saw one.'

'Nonsense', said Wrench. ''Tis true!' insisted Hernaman. 'Well, come on, who was it then?' asked the reverend. 'Mrs Parker, of all people,' replied Hernaman, and Wrench then told his friend that the lady was, even then, gravely ill at her home. Mrs Parker was a poor widow whom Hernaman saw every Sunday at church, where she volunteered. She knew the housekeeper of Salvador House and sometimes helped out there if many guests were being entertained. With her quiet, gentle manners, she appealed greatly to Hernaman, who would often visit her in the kitchen, telling her how she reminded him of his late mother, and 'more than once I caressingly stroked her hair'.

THE CHECKED SHAWL

The headmaster worked all that day as usual and forgot about the 'ghost'. That night he slept deeply but again woke up suddenly, just before the chimes of 1.45am. He felt immediately the same intense dread creeping up his body and knew that, if he turned in his bed, the figure would be there again. It was.

The next morning, Hernaman came downstairs to a message, asking him to go and visit Mrs Parker as soon as possible. On arrival, she was in a trance-like calm. 'There she lay on her little bed – so clean and tidy.' She at once recognized his voice, and a 'pleased smile of restful satisfaction' played over her face. He read to her from the Bible for a while, then got up to leave, but noticed one difference in her figure from the apparition – there was no checked shawl. Giving no reason for his question, he asked her sister, who was nursing her, if she ever wore a checked shawl. 'Why,' she exclaimed, 'do you mean this?' She brought out, from a box near the bed's head, the very shawl Hernaman had seen, explaining that it was put around the patient's shoulders to keep her warm – in the small hours.

TICK TOCK: FALLING IN LOVE WITH BIG BEN

✦ ✦ ✦

ig Ben is the climax of London's stormy love affair with Father Time. London's symbol is a clock because London was the ordered, imperial and railway capital. Humanity really only counted time in minutes when 'railway time' came along; before then, we never needed such precision. In Victorian London, being in a rush became almost a boast. The White Rabbit in *Alice in Wonderland* (1865), always late and with a huge watch, was a satire on contemporary man.

THE TYRANNY OF THE CLOCK

Until late Tudor times, a clock with two hands was almost unknown. Shakespeare's parents had never heard a ticking clock. In Tudor London, there were almost no domestic clocks and only 100 or so church clocks.

Time is a big theme with Shakespeare, because it was suddenly becoming more intrusive: Richard II in prison muses that he has become 'a numbering clock', and time seems to madden Macbeth as it 'creeps on' with its 'petty pace until the last syllable of recorded time'. To the modern-day director Nicholas Hytner, Macbeth was 'stuck in a vast ticking mechanism'. Shakespeare, writing in London as the Lord Chamberlain was dictating play times to prevent a clash with Mass, must have longed for the lazy days of his poaching childhood: 'There's no clock in the forest,' says a character in *As You Like It*.[1]

AUGUSTUS PUGIN

Londoners generally did most things, including walking and talking, faster than other Britons. This city in a hurry grew to love clocks. The 1851 Great Exhibition in Hyde Park was dominated by a whopper, which now sits on top of King's Cross Station. But, as George III, an obsessive clock-mender, demonstrated, a love of clocks can be close to madness. Big Ben, that symbol of enduring stability, was the work of two very unstable 'clockophiles': a genius lunatic and a savant sociopath.

AS GEORGE III, AN OBSESSIVE CLOCK-MENDER, DEMONSTRATED, A LOVE OF CLOCKS CAN BE CLOSE TO MADNESS.

Augustus Pugin was the architect of the clock tower. Forever in overdrive, Pugin was a draughtsman by the age of 14, running a business by 19 and dead at 40, having designed scores of buildings and written books insisting that architecture must be 'a romantic moral force'. He hated to see mankind turned into drones by the Industrial Revolution, so he loved things to be made by hand.[2]

He fell in love as easily as he wept: often. Here he is in his prime: 'a massive forehead, quick, pale grey eyes, a sonorous trumpet voice and long dark hair'. When working well, he sang opera in a loud baritone, swearing filthily when things went awry. He habitually dressed in a greasy sailor's jacket, with loose pilot's trousers, jackboots and 'a wide-awake hat'. 'So you see the sort of man he was,' said John Betjeman in a 1952 wireless talk, 'unconventional, downright humorous, an intense individualist who loved people'.

His greatest work was his co-design for the Houses of Parliament. Although the architect Charles Barry claimed most of the credit, Pugin, with his incredible speed and versatility, designed and oversaw most of the interior, from the great throne in the House of Lords down to elaborate letterboxes and door handles.

As his final illness, probably syphilis, affected his body and mind, he was still overworking, slaving on panelling and carpets for the long-running Parliament project. To the despair of his third wife Jane, his normal shift was 6am until 10pm, but he was increasingly plagued by visions and 'mind mists'. Slipping in and out of insanity, a committee of his friends decided to commit him to 'Bedlam', the dreadful Bethlem Royal Hospital in Lambeth (the building, with grim irony, is now a museum to two world wars, the Imperial War Museum).

THE BELL TOWER

Just before Pugin was committed, a letter from Charles Barry arrived, imploring help with the final problem at Westminster: a clock. Pugin rose to the challenge and, as he wrote in one of his last letters, 'never worked so hard'. Of his bell tower design, he said, in an eerie echo of Richard II in prison, 'It is beautiful, and I am become the whole machinery of the clock' – meaning that he worked so hard that, in his madness, he almost became the clock. How fitting that, with his great desire to benefit his fellow man, Pugin's final design was the most loved building in Britain. Happily, at the end his wife got him out of Bedlam and back home. As they sat together in the garden at Ramsgate, he uttered almost his last words to her: 'It's a beautiful place, is it not?'

EDMUND DENISON: CLOCK DESIGNER

Despite Pugin's strange identification with the clock, he only designed the clock tower and dials. The actual clock was designed by Edmund Denison, an entertainingly combative baronet who still dressed in clothing of the Regency period. This gruff northerner was so abrasive that the College of Horologists only elected him president on the condition that he would never attend their lunches. Denison took after his father, who once publicly called a fellow nobleman a blackguard on the platform of Derby station. 'Brusque' is the kindest epithet I can find about him.

Taken on as an horological consultant by Sir Charles Barry, the architect in overall charge of the Parliament rebuild, Denison quickly accused him of corruption in appointing his crony, Benjamin Vulliamy, as the clock's designer. Although Vulliamy was the Queen's clockmaker, Denison called his design 'a large village clock' and hounded him off the project. The furious Vulliamy published Denison's bilious letters in full and proceeded to a quiet retirement, collecting old clocks and enjoying the company of his three children.

DENISON'S FEUD WITH AIRY

Denison's next victim was Sir George Airy, a man from an uneducated Suffolk farm-labouring family who rose to be Astronomer Royal, who had set out standards for the clock to meet. Denison declared that Airy was not qualified to oversee the clock's design. Although it was Airy who demanded that the clock be accurate to a second, and checked by the Greenwich Observatory twice daily, his knowledge of clockmaking was, Denison said, 'purely theoretical'.

In 1850 Denison's *Rudimentary Treatise on Clocks, Watches and Bells* was published by Crosby and Lockwood, an obscure firm in Ludgate Circus. It quickly became the standard work, but embedded in its abstruse technical information was a demolition of Airy. The contents include 'Airy's conclusions erroneous' and 'Correction of Airy's mistakes'. The author wrote of 'some enemies' who told the press that Big Ben was controlled from Airy's office at the Greenwich Observatory, whereas it was merely checked by Greenwich, with impressive results. (Even in 1940, when bombs destroyed the cabling which communicated Big

EVEN IN 1940, WHEN BOMBS DESTROYED THE CABLING WHICH COMMUNICATED BIG BEN'S ACCURACY TO GREENWICH, THE CLOCK HAD NOT ERRED MORE THAN TWO SECONDS IN A YEAR, SO THAT THE CABLING WAS NEVER RECONNECTED.

Ben's accuracy to Greenwich, the clock had not erred more than two seconds in a year, so that the cabling was never reconnected.)

Worn down, Airy resigned from the Big Ben design project. Unfortunately, and to Denison's glee, Airy was later partly blamed for the Tay Bridge disaster, having advised its engineers over-optimistically. He went on to initiate the transatlantic telegraph, work on early computers, and write some not-contemptible poetry and a pioneering study of migraine, based on his own sufferings. He died in 1881, the father of nine children.

Other contents headings in the *Treatise on Clocks* include: 'Baily's mistake', 'Loseby's spring mechanism fails', 'Eminent firms' frauds', and 'The French metre a bad measure'.

FEUDING WITH BARRY

Denison's most epic battle was with the supervising architect of Parliament, the man who had rashly hired him, Charles Barry. Their feud lasted sixteen years, and the *Treatise* laid out Denison's position forensically. Barry's interference in designing the clock hands was 'very bad', and their weight contributed to the epic delay of the project. Two men could wind the clock once a week but oh no, Barry had all sorts of ideas for it to be automatically wound. The most enjoyable Barry idea, which would have been an ecological wonder, was for the commuters streaming over Westminster Bridge to power the clock by their footsteps. A section of the bridge would be a sort of hydraulic weighbridge.

'Any intelligent reader,' the *Treatise* sneered – and here he threatens us from the grave – 'can see the absurdity of Barry's ideas.' Interestingly, the one collaborator for whom Denison had kind words was Pugin. The two driven 'clockophiles' were kindred spirits. Denison died, childless, in 1905, and even caused aggravation from the grave, leaving a will so complex that it caused years of litigation.

THE BELL

Technically Big Ben is, of course, the huge bell in the clock tower, which sixteen horses hauled to Parliament Square from the barge that delivered it, not the clock. And it is not named after Sir Benjamin Hall, a boring Parliamentary official, but after Benjamin Caunt, the 114kg (18st) landlord of the Coach and Horses pub in St Martin's Lane and a much-loved boxer, who died just as Big Ben became operational.

Although Denison fought a two-year libel suit with George Mears, the bellfounder, alleging that the bell had holes in it that had been filled in with coloured bell-dust, its chime still comforts millions and it really is true that, in certain weather conditions, it has been heard at Windsor Castle in Berkshire.

The accuracy of the clock after all these years is no myth either, even after wartime bombs, a workman leaving his hammer in the works, and the 23cm (9in) lean inflicted on the tower by tunnelling underneath to build the Jubilee Line. The tower even sways, very slowly, to and fro with different temperatures. The only adjustment needed, as the designer directed, is to change the number of old pennies on the pendulum mechanism. Denison, beastliness aside, managed to achieve Airy's desired accuracy. Big Ben chimed throughout the Blitz, and its bells are still transmitted live for BBC news broadcasts via a microphone in the tower.

Big Ben is an icon of Victorian engineering, but also a monument to the eccentrics who made it.

Notes

1. Neil MacGregor, *Shakespeare's Restless World*, BBC Radio 4, 2012.
2. All my love of Pugin's tragic genius comes from Rosemary Hill's astonishingly enjoyable *God's Architect: Pugin and the Building of Romantic Britain* (Allen Lane, 2007).

RED ANNIE AND ELEANOR MARX

✦　✦　✦

L ondon's turn-of-the-century women freedom fighters have been strangely neglected, considering their role in both getting women the vote and securing workers' rights. Eleanor Marx (Karl Marx's daughter), Annie Besant and Emmeline Pankhurst are extraordinary figures of whom any city should be proud, but the stupendous 1,000-page *London Encyclopaedia* (2010) gives their ground-breaking activities eight lines, less than Arsenal football club.

ELEANOR MARX

Eleanor Marx's house still exists, but a blue plaque was only put on it in 2008. There is a video, posted online by the Sydenham Society, of the plaque unveiling ceremony in a suburban back garden. It is raining steadily, and the few short speeches are moving. Eleanor was a woman of epic courage. She was reared in a cramped flat in Dean Street, Soho, which is now above an expensive restaurant. Life there is best described by

the legendary Marxist scholar Eric Hobsbawm, whom
I spoke with a couple of times – imagine a punctilious and
ascerbic voice:

> *The squalor in which the Marxes – six persons – lived in*
> *their two furnished rooms in Soho was vividly described by*
> *visiting Prussian police spies, and the daily Dickensian struggle*
> *with butchers, bakers, landlords, and pawnbrokers emerges in*
> *Marx's correspondence with the ever loyal Engels, on whose financial*
> *aid he now relied permanently. Three of the Marx children died*
> *during these terrible years and were buried in the churchyard of*
> *Whitefield's Tabernacle in Tottenham Court Road, Mrs Marx having*
> *to beg £2 from a neighbouring French political refugee to pay for the*
> *coffin of one of them. Not surprisingly Jenny Marx's nerves often*
> *gave way, as did Karl's hardly equable temper. 'At home a constant*
> *state of siege' he reported to Engels in 1851; 'Am annoyed and*
> *enraged by streams of tears all night long ... I'm sorry for my wife.*
> *She bears the brunt of the pressure, and* au fond *she is right.*
> *In spite of this ... from time to time I lose my temper.'[1]*

ELEANOR'S EARLY LIFE

Karl Marx spent most days at the British Museum nearby,
researching *Das Kapital*. He was a creature of habit – always at
seat 07 in the reading room – and an old-fashioned father. When
Eleanor fell in love at 17 with a man twice her age, whom she
met in Paris, the flamboyant Basque revolutionary Hippolyte
Lissagaray, he forbade her to see him. It says much for his power
that the revolution-minded girl obeyed. Marx was lucky in his
daughter. Not only was she academically gifted and, her mother
said, 'political from head to toe', but she loyally gave up nearly
a decade to nurse her infirm father until his death. She reflected

later: 'I sacrificed the best, precious years of my life.' As his executor, she had to deal with his estate: £250.

Despite this long distraction, her political education was positively cinematic: touring Ireland with Marx's fellow theorist Engels, helping refugees escape bloody repression in Paris in 1871 and being arrested there, participating in the dawn of socialism with Shaw and Morris, and spending much of her time in the East End of London. There she fought anti-Semitism and supported the dockers' strike.

WOMEN'S RIGHTS

Eleanor's books, *Factory Hell* (1885) and *The Woman Question* (1886) had more immediate impact than her father's. Realizing that Ibsen's plays, such as *A Doll's House*, could dramatically show the housewife's lot, Eleanor learned Norwegian and became his first translator into English. She even staged the play, with George Bernard Shaw and herself in leading roles. Flaubert's *Madame Bovary* similarly championed an independent-minded woman and its first English translation, in 1886, was by Eleanor. Released by Karl's death, she became friends with the now married Lissagaray and translated his *History of the Paris Commune*.

Like her father, Eleanor worked long hours in the British Museum's reading room, a haven of gender equality – nearly: 'I saw Eleanor in the Museum yesterday [wrote a friend to the novelist Olive Schreiner]. She fairly danced with anger; the translation of the *Kama Sutra* is locked up, refused to women.' In 1883 the world of Mrs Tiggy-Winkle collided with Marxism. Prim Beatrix Potter met Eleanor in the museum tearoom and wrote: 'She has peculiar views on love and probably enjoys "natural" relations with men. She has a comely figure, dressed in a slovenly picturesque way with black hair flying about. Fine eyes, full of life and sympathy, otherwise ugly, complexion showing the signs of an unhealthy excited life, kept up with stimulants and narcotics.'[2]

With her Frida Kahlo-like face and black mane, she was a spellbinding orator at rallies on women's rights and labour rights. If 'labour rights' sounds boring, Eleanor was partly responsible for the limited eight-hour day which we are all entitled to (even if we choose not to go home at its end); her rousing speech on this subject sold in thousands as a pamphlet.

A SAD END

Eleanor's personal life, however, descended into a Plath-esque abyss. She fell in love and lived with Edward Aveling, a Stoke Newington physics teacher who embodied many of man's worst features. A crook and compulsive philanderer, he was widely disliked. 'A little lizard of a man', recalled William Morris's daughter. The couple lived at 55 Great Russell Street, just opposite the British Museum, before buying a large house in Sydenham, which she christened the 'Den'.

As 'Alec Nelson', Aveling secretly married a young actress, set up house with her in Stafford Mansions, Albert Bridge Road, Battersea, and informed Eleanor by letter. Although he returned to Eleanor when he became seriously ill, making her a reluctant nurse twice over, her heart was broken. She dutifully pushed Aveling around Sydenham in a bath chair. Her old friend Engels deepened her grief, taking over the publication of Karl's posthumous work, and claiming paternity of her beloved brother Fred. In 1898, upstairs in the back room at 7 Jew's Walk, Sydenham, she took prussic acid and killed herself, aged 43:

Now boast thee Death, in thy possession lies a lass unparalleled.[3]

After this, Aveling returned to Eva, his young wife, and died four months later at Stafford Mansions in Battersea. Thirteen years after Eleanor's death, her sister Laura Marx killed herself in Paris, with prussic acid (cyanide).

ANNIE BESANT

Eleanor had joined Annie Besant – Red Annie – in encouraging 1,500 women to walk out of the toxic Bryant and May match factory at Bow, east London. The 1888 match girls' strike was a milestone in both women's and labour history. Like Eleanor, Annie was born in the visceral heart of London, on Fish Street Hill, by Billingsgate Market. An even more electrifying orator than Eleanor, Annie was as clever. Even the fellow socialist Beatrice Webb told her 'You have read too much.' She fought the women's struggle at several mass rallies; one in Hyde Park attracted 145,000 women, and she spoke at the original 'Bloody Sunday' meeting in Trafalgar Square.

Here, on a winter day in 1887, workers gathered to protest against unemployment. Although 2,000 police were present, the government sent in the army as well. A total of 75 protesters were injured by truncheon blows and the hooves of cavalry horses; one protester was bayoneted. Annie tried to get arrested, but police had special instructions not to create such a prominent martyr.

Soon after this, she published birth-control information and two court actions followed: the first a prosecution for pornography, the second to transfer custody of her children to her ex-husband. Unable to get into politics – even the London County Council barred women – Annie went to India, where she died in 1933, a heroine of the Indian independence movement, as hated by the men who ran the Raj as she had been feared by the men who ran London.

EMMELINE PANKHURST

Eleanor and Annie paved the way for the long suffragette campaign, which ran from extensive offices near the Strand. The site is now part of the left-leaning London School of Economics, a nice psycho-geographical match. The hero of that campaign was Emmeline Pankhurst, whose political education had started very young: reading the morning paper to her father over breakfast.

At the age of 5 she collected pennies for slaves in America and at 30 she was living at 8 Russell Square, a radical hub much visited by the founding fathers of socialism. Emmeline joined Eleanor and Annie in supporting the match girls' strike and was repeatedly imprisoned for her violent protests, which included a day of smashing London shop windows. She showed heroic stamina in Holloway Prison as a hunger striker and by a refusal to sleep, but her little sister Mary was less robust and died as a result of force-feeding there. Through all this, Emmeline struggled with poverty and the death of her husband and two little boys (diphtheria and polio). She ploughed on with her charismatic public speeches, at one of which £14,000 was raised.

A journalist described Emmeline: Parisian in dress style ever since an early stay there, with olive skin, flushed a little red in the cheeks and with delicately pencilled eyebrows above striking violet-blue eyes. She died at 43 Wimpole Street, just north of Oxford Street. There is no plaque on the house, but in 1998 one was put up a few doors away, dedicated to Sir Evelyn Baring, a forgotten British imperialist.

SYLVIA PANKHURST

Emmeline's daughter Sylvia was an accomplished artist, and another frequently imprisoned and force-fed socialist suffragette. Deeply involved in helping East End workers, in 1913 she co-founded a cooperative factory there with a free day nursery.

With her Italian lover, she moved to Woodford Green, near the northern end of the Central Line, and opened a transport café. She lived until 1960, so there are oral memories of her online, and although her house has been demolished, there is a strange Pankhurst legacy in an overgrown thicket in Woodford: Sylvia's anti-war sculpture, recently restored.

A LASTING LEGACY

One site that is never neglected is Emmeline's grave in Brompton cemetery, South Kensington, which always has fresh flowers on it, placed by visitors from all over the world. In 1928, after she and Eleanor Marx had died, and Annie was living in Madras, all women got the vote.

Notes

1. Eric Hobsbawm, 'Karl Marx' in the *Oxford Dictionary of National Biography* (Oxford University Press, 2004).

2. Susan Bernstein, *Roomscape: Women Writers at the British Museum from George Eliot to Virginia Woolf* (Edinburgh University Press, 2013) pp.38–40. *The Kama Sutra* was the new Richard Burton translation.

3. Charmian on Cleopatra, Shakespeare, Antony and Cleopatra Act V, scene ii. Engels confessed just before he died that Fred was the son of Karl and the housekeeper, and that he, Engels, had only claimed paternity to protect the great name of Marx. Just how great that name became is proved by Stalin's personal intervention, to bury the truth of this Marx love child.

PASSIONATE INTENSITY AT THE NATURAL HISTORY MUSEUM

✦ ✦ ✦

We all love the huge blue whale model, and the long-tailed dinosaur dominating the entrance hall – which is affectionately called Mr Whippy (or similar). And of course the Gothic building is a stylistic one-off, with all those carved beasts and shells. The ceiling paintings of ancient plants are neglected masterpieces; I once saw the poet Sir John Betjeman just staring up at them, lost in Carboniferous reverie and oblivious of the crowds, in the pose of his statue at St Pancras Station.

But the staff of this museum repay closer study, as much as the specimens. The hothouse atmosphere of this great research institution has bred some truly exotic human psychologies. Since my youth, I have cycled there with specimens to be identified, partly for the thrill of going behind those polished mahogany doors to meet the nature boffins, with their windows overlooking secret courtyards.

MOLLUSCS, INSECTS AND BIRDS

Specialization-induced eccentricity started early on, even before the zoology collection moved out of the British Museum. The Regency-era keeper George Shaw sold off specimens that did not concern his specialization. His successor, William Leach, a mollusc man, held regular bonfires of non-*Mollusca*. Leach's lack of imagination was also displayed by his naming 27 new species after a close male friend, John Cranch.

Periodically, and amusingly, nepotism cut through the specialists. In 1862, for instance, a trustee's relation got a job in 'Insects', despite not knowing the difference between a moth and a butterfly. As late as 1935, public schoolboy James Macdonald, by his own admission 'knowing nothing about birds', joined 'Ornithology' (he did blossom into a great expert, however).

> THE REGENCY-ERA KEEPER GEORGE SHAW SOLD OFF SPECIMENS THAT DID NOT CONCERN HIS SPECIALIZATION. HIS SUCCESSOR, WILLIAM LEACH, A MOLLUSC MAN, HELD REGULAR BONFIRES OF NON-MOLLUSCA.

The most famous specialist 'case' was the Edwardian forerunner of Kafka, W. N. P. Barbellion, who toiled for years in the Insect Room before writing the sensationally downbeat *Journal of a Disappointed Man* (1919), with H. G. Wells's enthusiastic introduction. Disappointed or not, Barbellion's work on lice was crucial to easing soldiers' discomfort in the First World War.

MAMMALS, MOSQUITOES AND SHELLFISH

Mammal man Oldfield Thomas had no such creative outlet for his sense of isolation. Retirement in 1923, and then the death of his wife, troubled him greatly. He carried on coming to work, unpaid. But in 1929, aged 71, he sat at his desk and killed himself with a handgun.

Very many other keepers have been happily workaholic, or devoted to a noble cause, depending on your perspective. Mosquito man Peter Mattingly was so eminent that an African visitor, finding him out of the office, asked if he could just see the great man's desk. Mattingly, hump-backed from decades of microscope work, came to work as usual one summer morning, only to be followed by his wife in a state of agitation. The family were going on holiday that morning: Mattingly had simply forgotten and gone to work on autopilot. Similarly, shellfish man Ellis Owen was still productively coming to work in 2008, aged 84.

FOSSILS AND BEETLES

A 1930s fossil keeper called Leslie Bairstow was as famous for his unproductivity. He was so eminent as a youth that, when he was hired, another keeper ran through the corridors shouting 'We've got Bairstow! We've got Bairstow!' But he proceeded to publish nothing. Bairstow became, according to the keeper Richard Fortey in his wonderful book *The Secret Life of the Natural History Museum*, an obsessive cataloguer, even of the pieces of string used on parcels he was sent. These he boxed by length, and one was labelled 'Pieces of string too short to be of use'.

This autistic spectrum conduct is an occupational hazard of the dedication required in a world where, for instance, rove beetle expert Peter Hamilton can only distinguish many species by a microscopic look at their genitalia.

DARK AND DEVIOUS

Distinguished botanist Herbert Wernham's cataloguing inclination took a darker route. After his death, a card index was found at the museum recording the prostitutes he had visited, with a sprig of their pubic hair pinned to each card. Poor Wernham, who had sustained mental trauma during the First World War, retired in 1921. Modern-day museum botanist William Stearns, after much detective work, discovered that, after a spell in Hanwell Asylum, he died in 1941, an alcoholic.

An opposite, extrovert and outdoor character was Colonel Richard Meinertzhagen (1878–1967), spy and war hero (see box). As a boy he knew Charles Darwin. As a soldier, Lawrence of Arabia was his friend, but noted his instability (pot, kettle, black). The aristocratic colonel cut a striking figure in his black cloak, which he even wore for table tennis, and brought in so many specimens that he was given the run of the museum and made an honorary associate. He lived around the corner, so was a frequent visitor.

> The colonel invited my Arabic-speaking father, Regimental Sergeant Major Leslie Latham, on an expedition to Arabia in search of raptors. Dad was always wistful that, being in love with my mother, he did not accept.

Only in recent years has his breathtaking fraud been exposed by museum experts. Several museum specimens, such as a Blyth's kingfisher supposedly from Burma, were simply stolen by the colonel from the museum and re-presented. He was one of those odd coves who are genuinely remarkable – he really was a great naturalist who discovered new species – but had a compulsion, driven by an impish joy in trouncing everyday folk, to fantasize. It gave him a low-level version of the thrill he got from war.

DEDICATED WOMEN

Nowadays, and probably to the reader's relief, many more women populate the museum's staff, thanks in part to two pioneers. Dorothea Bate started aged 19 in 1898 and stayed 50 years, an intrepid fossil hunter revered by the great Leakey. And Joan Proctor, who took a crocodile to school in Hammersmith and wrote her first scientific paper at 19, overcame lifelong ill-health to become a world authority on reptiles and a great popularizer of science. She died in 1931, but a bust of her in London Zoo reminds us of the more socially adjusted alumni of the Natural History Museum.

FLINGING A POT OF PAINT IN THE FACE OF THE PUBLIC

✦ ✦ ✦

This is what John Ruskin, the self-appointed custodian of Victorian taste, thought of the painter James Whistler: 'I have seen much of cockney impudence before now, but I never expected to hear a coxcomb ask 200 guineas for flinging a pot of paint in the face of the public.' *Punch* magazine was as tough on Whistler's *Nocturne*: 'all inky flood'.

There is something about London that inspired – or at least unleashed – visionary painters – radical, crazy, unprecedented painters. The secret is in Shelley's line on London, 'That great sea that still howls for more'. These artists were talented anyway, but living in London knocked down the walls of their minds and removed 'the mind-forg'd manacles' (Blake) or, in Francis Bacon's phrase, 'opened the valves of feeling'.

JAMES GILLRAY

Take James Gillray, for instance. Born in sleepy Milman's Row, Chelsea (it is still sleepy), as a little boy he drew a beautifully accurate goldfinch (now in the British Museum) and went on to emulate the dreary fashion dictated by Sir Joshua Reynolds for paintings designed to raise morals. But he became incapable of doing a straight portrait. Caricature crept in and became extreme.

Gillray, a manic depressive, was incapable of boring pictures. Politicians were viciously drawn in a way that directly inspired the makers of the Spitting Image puppets in the 1980s. A Frenchman recorded that when new cartoons

A FRENCHMAN RECORDED THAT WHEN NEW CARTOONS APPEARED IN THE WINDOW OF A GALLERY AT 3 PICCADILLY, YOU HAD TO FIGHT THROUGH THE CROWD WITH YOUR FISTS TO SEE THEM.

appeared in the window of a gallery at 3 Piccadilly, you had to fight through the crowd with your fists to see them. After he drew Prime Minister Pitt as a toadstool on a dunghill, Pitt paid him a pension to mute his satire. Gillray took the pension but carried on demolishing politicians. For *More Pigs than Teats*, with its cross-party array of corrupt politicians all jostling for personal gain, he risked his liberty, but the king loved it.

Never rich, he lodged for his last twenty years with Hannah Humphrey, over the shop in St James's Street where she sold his pictures. A touching couple, they once got to the door of St James's Church in Piccadilly in wedding garb before Gillray got cold feet and turned back. Knowing his forgetfulness, she once wrote to him when away, 'Pray don't forget to feed the cat.'

There are still plenty of books on society painters but virtually none on Gillray, because the Victorians tried to bury his reputation. Fishwives thrashing bare-bottomed nuns, and frequent images of buggery, flagellation and lechery were too much until a 2001 Tate exhibition reinstated him as the father of satire and a sort of proto-Francis Bacon with laughs.

THOMAS ROWLANDSON

A later caricaturist whose works were also sold by Hannah Humphrey was Thomas Rowlandson, born in Old Jewry, a short, one-way street near the Mansion House, now full of banks. His cartoons of London life and politics were obscene, very funny and often at the expense of lecherous old men; he too entered obscurity until the twentieth century.

He lived in a series of shabby flats around Soho: 103 Wardour Street, 50 Poland Street, then a basement in the Strand, then with the alcoholic Soho-born painter George Morland (a neglected master of bucolic scenes, which can be seen in Tate Britain). He finally came to rest in an attic near Charing Cross, where he lived from 1800 until his unremarked death in 1827.

HENRY FUSELI

After the Swiss artist Henry Fuseli married Sophia Rawlins at St Mary's Church in Marylebone in 1788, he lived in Foley Street, near Goodge Street Tube, until his death in 1825. The Scottish philosopher Hume called him 'mad as Rousseau himself' – Fuseli had visited the French freethinker in Paris. He was indeed unlike any artist before or since, and his paintings have an Edgar Allen Poe-style power to disturb.

Everybody knows Fuseli's *The Nightmare* (Tate Britain), with its evil imp and wild-eyed horse above a sleeping, ravished-looking woman. In the same gallery can be seen his *Incubus* picture, of a demon flying out of a window and leaving an exhausted woman. This is a realistic portrayal of a horrific visitation that happened to a woman of my acquaintance, someone who had never heard of an incubus but described its (doubtless psychosomatic) effect with sheer terror.

Fuseli's use of dreams and the unconscious has made him a hero to surrealists and Freudians. London still hides his genius, like a suppressed nightmare: in vain I used to submit written requests to see his banned erotica (which was in the catalogue) in the old British Museum reading room. Similarly, Ruskin told the Victorian world that he had burned sheaves of Turner's erotic pictures; in fact he had merely buried them in a labyrinthine cataloguing system. They were rediscovered in Tate Britain in 2004. Ruskin was famously prudish. It was probably in his Park Street, Mayfair house that he ran from his wife's bedside, horrified at the existence of pubic hair.

LONDON STILL HIDES HIS GENIUS, LIKE A SUPPRESSED NIGHTMARE: IN VAIN I USED TO SUBMIT WRITTEN REQUESTS TO SEE HIS BANNED EROTICA (WHICH WAS IN THE CATALOGUE) IN THE OLD BRITISH MUSEUM READING ROOM.

WILLIAM BLAKE

Fuseli was close to William Blake, arguably the most visionary of all London artists and one who rarely left London, but saw the cosmos on its streets and angels at Peckham Rye. His thread of social commentary on London's poor was positively Dickensian.

For Soho-born Blake, London contained heaven and hell and he passed happy hours sitting naked in his south London back garden, conversing with deities or with his illiterate wife Catherine. They were married at St Mary's Church, Battersea, which is still like a country church nestling quietly on the riverside.

Like all the cockney visionary artists, Blake began with conventional subjects before drawing in his own unique pilgrim-mystic style. Many agreed with Wordsworth in calling him mad, but Catherine was his lifelong supporter, even though she sometimes put an empty plate in front of him to demonstrate their poverty.

I only know one person (my eccentric older brother) who has read Edward Young's epic poem *Night Thoughts on Life, Death and Immortality* and unfortunately Blake accepted a commission to illustrate it. He did 537 painstaking watercolours before the publisher went bust; he never even got the measly £21 he had been offered. In 1809 he exhibited his pictures in Broad Street, Soho. They were pronounced 'hideous' and none sold. Even his beautiful hand-coloured book, *Jerusalem*, now priceless and containing the hymn we all know of, remained unsold at his death.

I ONLY KNOW ONE PERSON (MY ECCENTRIC OLDER BROTHER) WHO HAS READ EDWARD YOUNG'S EPIC POEM *NIGHT THOUGHTS ON LIFE, DEATH AND IMMORTALITY* AND UNFORTUNATELY BLAKE ACCEPTED A COMMISSION TO ILLUSTRATE IT. HE DID 537 PAINSTAKING WATERCOLOURS BEFORE THE PUBLISHER WENT BUST.

Getting older, Blake took to rising in the night and working for two or three hours, his faithful Catherine by his side. It now seems that this gardener's daughter had an unrecognized role in

Blake's artwork, being a practical engraver and a competent artist herself. She probably finished his Bunyan illustrations after his death. Her good humour is attested by her comment: 'I rarely see Mr Blake, he is so often in Paradise.' Even her illiteracy may be a myth. It is based solely on her signing the marriage register at Battersea with a cross, a common practice for those without a copperplate script.

The Blakes ended their days together in two rooms off the Strand. There William died in a state of bliss: 'Just before he died his countenance became fair and he burst out singing of the Things he saw in Heaven.' Good luck awaited Catherine. The perennially eccentric but discerning Wyndham family came to the rescue: Lord Egremont bought Blake's illustrations of *The Faerie Queen* for 80 guineas, which sustained Catherine for the short remaining tenure of her life. Posthumously Blake has a worldwide reputation and, a mile from his impoverished final rooms in the Strand, a monumental statue of his engraving of Isaac Newton dominates the forecourt of the new British Library building at St Pancras.

JOHN MARTIN

Like Blake, Chelsea resident John Martin was called 'mad' in his lifetime. Until the late twentieth century, he was disregarded: his large *The Last Judgement* was sold in 1935 for £7, and cut up for fire screens. Martin, the thirteenth child of a tanner, was normal by family standards: one brother was a fanatical Methodist arsonist who set York Minster on fire, another a prophet who exhibited a perpetual-motion machine in London in 1808.

Martin painted vast scenes of apocalyptic moments in history and the Bible with cinematic detail. His *Destruction of Sodom and*

Gomorrah captured the cities in mid-air, about to fall into a void. Canvases such as *The Destruction of Pompeii*, *Bridge Over Chaos* and *Belshazzar's Feast*, scorned by the Royal Academy, were real crowd-pleasers, the Victorian equivalent of Imax 3D cinema.

Long after Martin's death in 1854, he inspired a new wave of artists – the directors of *Star Wars* and *Blade Runner* were especially influenced, as the 2012 Tate Gallery exhibition on John Martin demonstrated.

JOSEPH MALLORD WILLIAM TURNER

Within a mile of Blake's birthplace and eighteen years later, J. M. W. Turner was born in Maiden Lane, Covent Garden. Although for many years he painted conventional 'views' of buildings and landscapes, evocative light effects were always evident, and it was to experience weather effects fully that he famously had himself lashed to a main mast for four hours in a storm. He insisted that his paintings in the National Gallery be hung next to those of his hero, Claude Lorrain (1600–82). Although this wish was not respected for many decades, it has now been fulfilled. Looking at the masters together, you can understand Turner's last words – 'The Sun is God.'

The more courtly John Constable dined with Turner once at the Royal Academy in Piccadilly and discovered a true cockney: 'He is uncouth but has a wonderful range of mind.' Although Turner, partly again through Lord Egremont's patronage, lived in tolerable comfort, he admitted that 'Had Tom Girtin lived, I'd have starved.'

THOMAS GIRTIN

The little-known Girtin, who died at 27, was born in Southwark, son of a Huguenot brush-maker. Working from his house in Long Acre, near today's Covent Garden Tube, Girtin seemed a bolder, more effortless version of Turner. Of his few works to survive, the *House at Chelsea* – a small, white cottage seen across a hallucinatory riverscape – is much reproduced. Sadly, his 33m (108ft) panorama of London has been lost. It is the biggest picture of London in history. The dashing, likeable Thomas Girtin died early, but happily married to Mary, the 16-year-old daughter of an Aldersgate goldsmith.

Together, the cockneys Girtin and Turner forged a new use of watercolour, and a new way of seeing. Their London heirs were Whistler, with his impressionist Thames studies, and in the twentieth century, Francis Bacon and Lucian Freud, the next wave of London painters to blow apart our ideas of beauty.

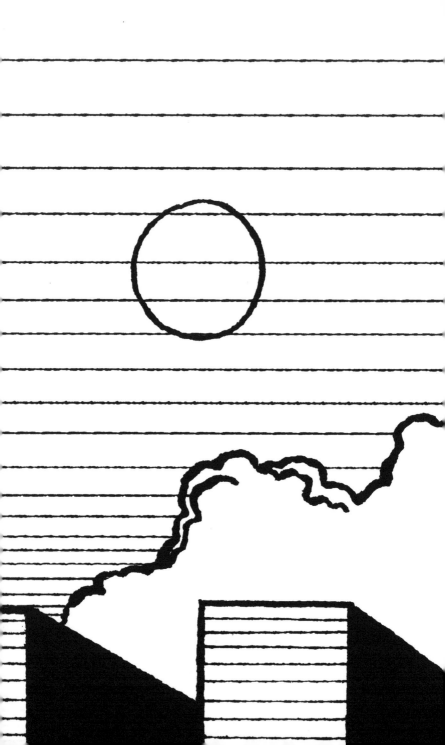

TWENTIETH-CENTURY
LONDON

TAKING TEA IN THE TOMB

✦ ✦ ✦

O rientalist and traveller Richard Burton, a friend said, 'looked like Othello and lived like the Three Musketeers blended into one'. Even more vividly, eroticist Frank Harris wrote:

I was at a London party, he was in conventional evening dress, but as he swung around to the introduction, there was an untamed air about him. Six feet tall, broad and square-shouldered, he carried himself like a young man. He was sixty, his face bronzed and scarred and his dark eyes were imperious and by no means friendly. He talked as only Burton could talk, of Damascus and the immemorial East, of India with its super-subtle people, of Africa and human life in the raw … and of his encyclopaedic reading, he knew English prose and poetry astonishingly; had a curious liking for the 'sabre-cuts of Saxon speech' – all such words as come hot from life's mint. His intellectual curiosity was astonishingly broad and deep, but deep down lay the despairing gloom of utter disbelief. Burton's laughter, deep-chested as it was, had in it something of sadness.[1]

Burton is best known for his unexpurgated translation, in sixteen volumes, of *The One Thousand and One Nights*, and for being the

first Westerner to visit Mecca. Disguised as an Arab, he even entered the room at the heart of the square, measured its interior and confirmed that the holy object within is a meteorite.

EXPLORER AND WRITER

Burton's energy was extraordinary – he spoke fifteen languages and published translations of Portuguese fiction, Hindu folk tales, and fourteen two-volume scholarly travelogues about the Levant, India, Africa, Iceland and Brazil. Anonymously, he penned the *Kasidah*, a still-readable long poem in Sufi style, celebrating Eastern languor and fatalism with panache and longing. An excellent swordsman whose fearlessness showed in his scarred face, his history of the sword remains definitive. His epic voyages to discover the source of the Nile failed in their object, but Burton did describe, for the first time, huge tracts of Central Africa.

His public feud with John Speke, his travelling companion in Africa, ran for years as each man claimed credit for discoveries in Africa and implied that the other had displayed cowardice in the face of native attacks.

ADVENTUROUS SEXUALITY

The abrasive streak in Burton affected his long marriage to
Isabel. She courted him for many years and insisted that she
was psychically connected to him. 'He was my earthly god!' she
gushed. Her new-age beliefs and fervent Roman Catholicism
repelled him. Conversely, she lamented his in-depth studies
of native sexual practices. He joyfully chronicled, often from
first-hand experiences, what he often regarded as superior sexual
technique in Africa and Asia. His documentation of male brothel
life got him into trouble with his army superiors.

Richard clandestinely translated and published the *Kama Sutra*,
but Isabel could not take it when he translated an even more
explicit and sexually inclusive work, the 1,000-page *The Perfumed
Garden*. The book remained in manuscript form only until after
Burton's death, when she was offered £6,000 for it by a publisher.
After three days of 'mental torture', Isabel concluded that, 'Out
of 1,500 men, 15 will read in the spirit of science', but 1,485
men would read it 'for filth's sake'. So, although she admitted it
was 'his *magnum opus*', she burnt it, 'sorrowfully, reverently'.
Afterwards, she almost expected him to rise up from the grave
and curse her. For this act she was widely condemned. Cornered,
she began to say that Richard's ghost had appeared to her and
instructed her to burn the book. Her final act of sanitization had
no such occult authorization.

DIARIES

The huge stack of Burton's diaries filled Isabel with fear. Far more
spontaneous and frank even than his books, the one surviving
volume shows that they were peppered with erotic digressions,

personal confessions and an overall respect for Eastern culture as superior to the Christian rigidity by which she lived. And she figured in a less than perfect role (in the *Nights* translation he had written of 'the cruelty of a good woman'). Although she publicly admired Richard as 'a spade-truth man', she felt it her duty 'to hide his faults from the public'. And so Isabel burned all the diaries that Richard had willed to her.

The poet Swinburne lashed out in verse at Isabel, and accused her of 'befouling Richard's memory like a harpy'. To female novelist and family friend, Ouida, Isabel had displayed 'the bigotry of the Inquisition's Torquemada, the vandalism of John Knox'. When

WHEN IT EMERGED THAT LADY BURTON HAD DRAGGED A PRIEST IN TO GIVE THE DYING RICHARD THE LAST RITES OF THE CATHOLIC FAITH, MANY OF HIS FRIENDS BROKE OFF ALL CONTACT WITH HER.

it emerged that Lady Burton had dragged a priest in to give the dying Richard the last rites of the Catholic faith, many of his friends broke off all contact with her.

For all that, we have cause to be grateful to Isabel, who supported and loved Richard for 30 years, nursed him devotedly, and wrote her own, often unintentionally revealing, accounts of their life and travels. But her final bizarre gesture to memorialize her husband's name might conceivably have summoned his ghost in anger.

THE STONE TENT

When Burton died, Isabel acted on a casual remark Burton had once made about them being buried together in a Bedouin tent, and had a stone tent erected to house their coffins in the Catholic cemetery at Mortlake, by the Thames near Barnes. Naturally enough, a big Catholic funeral was involved, attended by none of Burton's friends.

The tent is still there – hard to get to, but worth a visit as London's most bizarre tomb and a memorial to an unlikely marriage. Like the Ka'aba chamber at Mecca which Richard had penetrated all those years ago, only a few people have seen inside the tomb, but blurred photographs show a gilt casket for Richard and a mahogany one for his wife. A religious painting hangs on the wall and a jug on the floor is said to contain water from the holy well at Mecca, miraculously uncorrupted. Wires and electrics remain, relics of a kitsch mechanism that caused strings of camel bells inside to tinkle when the door was opened. Isabel used to sit inside the tomb-tent with friends and have tea in her husband's memory most Sundays. On four occasions, she held seances in the tent.

A NIECE'S PERSPECTIVE

Burton's niece, Georgiana Stisted, was particularly fond of
him and, appreciating his wild side, detested Isabel's possessive
hagiography. To Georgiana, Isabel, with her 'flimsy convent
education, excitable brain and deficient reasoning faculties'
was no fit wife for her uncle. In her own book, *The True Life
of Captain Richard Burton* (1897), Georgiana amusingly predicts
that 'Fifty years hence London's ever-advancing tide will have
swept away any vestige of the shabby cemetery where Richard
Burton lies.'

In one way (which would please Georgiana), London has been
unkind to the tomb. The huge stone crucifix on the front of the
tent, visible in early photographs, has gone.

Note
1. Quoted in Fawn Brodie, *The Devil Drives: A Life of Sir Richard Burton*
(Eyre & Spottiswoode, 1967), p.17.

THE SECRET OF
MILLIONAIRES' ROW

✦ ✦ ✦

Ian Cobain is a senior *Guardian* reporter, much awarded by
Amnesty International for his work on torture worldwide,
especially by Britain in Pakistan. In 2005 he got wind of
a completely unregulated wartime internment centre just off
Kensington High Street. Disturbingly, MI5's 'London Cage' was
not only a wartime facility: it remained in use until 1947. And,
even by wartime standards, its methods give us cause for national
shame. The Foreign Office blocked three freedom of information
requests by Cobain, but the shaven-headed Liverpudlian and
father of two persevered, and finally got the story, or part of it.[1]

FIRST WORLD WAR

MI5's interrogation of our enemies started back in 1914,
in a Cockfosters hut. Churchill, as Secretary for War, then
requisitioned the entire fifth floor of the Great Central Hotel
in Marylebone for interrogation. Guests entering the lift who
pressed the button for the fifth floor by mistake – which

happened frequently – were bundled back into the lift unceremoniously by military police.

CAMP 020

During the Second World War a large initial reception centre for captured enemy agents, codenamed Camp 020, was created in a mansion at Ham, near Richmond. Latchmere House is now private flats. In charge at this former lunatic asylum was a man who might have benefited from being sectioned himself (one of his officers thought him 'quite mad'). Colonel Robin Stephens, nicknamed 'Tin-Eye' from his permanent monocle, was a Raj veteran with brisk views: Belgians? 'Weepy and romantic.' The French? 'Corrupt.' Italians? 'Undersized and posturing.' Icelanders were 'unintelligent' and Jews 'shifty'.

At Camp 020, torture was routine, in 30 carpet-less cells. The job of the resident Dr Dearden was to keep inmates alive but to devise tortures, such as sleep deprivation and electrocution, which left no telltale marks.

THE CAGE

The most important prisoners were taken to the Cage in Kensington Palace Gardens for worse treatment. The street, known as Millionaires' Row, remains a gated community and the Cage is now partly flats and partly the Russian chancery. Here Stephens oversaw all the usual dreary litany of abuse we are used to shaking our heads over as practised by dictatorships or at Guantanamo Bay: mock executions, routine beatings, threats of amateur surgery, electric shocks, hair being pulled out, forcing prisoners to run endlessly with heavy weights, and frequent use of cold water immersion. Inmates routinely begged to be killed. As MI5's official historian has admitted, Britain is a world leader in this area.

One officer told an inmate, 'We are not bound by any rules. You leave here on a stretcher or in a hearse.' Cobain has found a paper by MI5's legal adviser pointing out that the Cage contravened the Geneva Convention and was in 'a legal void'. The advice was ignored. MI5 even kept the Cage secret from the government and the International Committee of the Red Cross. Then somebody blundered and included the Kensington address on a POW camp list given to the Red Cross. They visited twice, unannounced, but were turned away.

AFTER A FLURRY OF PANICKY MEMORANDA, INCLUDING THE ESTIMATE OF FOUR WEEKS TO REMOVE WHAT THEY CHILLINGLY CALLED 'INCRIMINATING GEAR', MI5 INVITED THE RED CROSS BACK AT AN APPOINTED TIME. THE GEAR WAS GONE, THE WALLS WERE SCRUBBED, AND THE MOST INCAPACITATED PRISONERS WERE TEMPORARILY SHIPPED OUT.

After a flurry of panicky memoranda, including the estimate of four weeks to remove what they chillingly called 'incriminating gear', MI5 invited the Red Cross back at an appointed time. The gear was gone, the walls were scrubbed, and the most incapacitated prisoners were temporarily shipped out. Only a few months earlier a horrified psychiatrist had visited and found a German naval officer in full dress uniform cleaning the floor with a toothbrush.

It was business as usual at the Cage until 1947 (the year *Gardeners' Question Time* began and Harold Wilson joined the Cabinet), only war criminals replaced suspected spies. The Cage grew out of the extremes of war, but surely the simplest evidence that it was not philosophically justifiable is the fact that the government still refuses to release the manuscript memoir of senior Cage official Colonel Scotland. Scotland submitted this to MI5 for approval in 1954 and, despite a recent request by the original publisher to get the full manuscript back, it remains in a locked vault at the National Archives in Kew, west London.

What of 'Tin-Eye' Stephens? He was court-martialled behind closed doors, and pleaded ignorance of the crimes on his watch, exactly as war criminals did at Nuremberg. He was acquitted.

Note

1. Ian Cobain, *Cruel Britannia* (Portobello Books, 2012). I have also used *MI9, Escape and Invasion 1939–1945* by M. R. D. Foot (Biteback, 1979) and *The Defence of the Realm: The Authorized History of MI5* by Christopher Andrew (Penguin, 2010).

LOST IN THE UNDERGROUND

✦ ✦ ✦

M yth and mystery surround London's 27 abandoned Tube stations. Increasingly, they are impossible to visit for security reasons, but you can find blurred photos on the Internet, taken by transport nerds from passing trains. One visitor to Drayton Park, a defunct station on the Northern Line, encountered gale-force winds of dry, warm air, propelled by nearby trains. Wind in a curved doorway produced an unnerving ghostly howl. Suddenly, the distant lights of a passing Victoria Line train flashed down a side tunnel.

There was a notable involuntary visitor to an abandoned station. An absent-minded commuter got off at South Kentish Town when the train was halted there at a signal. He was stuck there until he attracted attention by burning strips of advertising poster. John Betjeman wove a whole radio story around this unlucky man.

LITTLE KING WILLIAM STREET

The oldest 'ghost station', little King William Street, lasted just ten years, 1890–1900. It has a blue plaque as the site of the world's first electric underground railway. It is down by the river, which is reclaiming one of the old tunnels: it has stalactites on the ceiling and inches of Thames water on the trackbed. An ascending tunnel on the landward side of the station is now used to ventilate the Northern Line, which runs beneath it. On a platform at London Bridge, you can see ceiling vents that lead up to the abandoned tunnel.

In another station, a wartime 'Careless Talk Costs Lives' poster has been photographed *in situ* 60 years on. Poignant typewritten instructions to those sheltering from the Blitz remain: 'If you are leaving do not disturb others who are sleeping', recalling Henry Moore's eerie drawings of hundreds sleeping on Tube platforms.

ALDWYCH

Aldwych Station in the Strand is a well-known disused station, used in films such as *V for Vendetta* and *Atonement*. A listed building, its tiled façade bears its original name of Strand Station. Downstairs, a Tube map on the wall survives: Heathrow is not marked on it. During the Second World War, the Elgin Marbles were stored in Aldwych Station. These were the sculpted friezes from the Parthenon, the principal temple in Athens at the height of the golden age of Ancient Greece. What a trajectory they have had, from a Grecian sculptor's yard in 400 BC to the bright sun of the Parthenon pediment, then the sea voyage to the British Museum, where Keats wrote a sonnet on them, to a station 28m (92ft) under London. The precaution was wise – the Marbles' gallery in the museum sustained a direct hit during the Blitz.

WHAT A TRAJECTORY THEY HAVE HAD, FROM A GRECIAN SCULPTOR'S YARD IN 400 BC TO THE BRIGHT SUN OF THE PARTHENON PEDIMENT, THEN THE SEA VOYAGE TO THE BRITISH MUSEUM, WHERE KEATS WROTE A SONNET ON THEM, TO A STATION 28M (92FT) UNDER LONDON.

Here is a logic puzzle for those readers who like such things: how were the huge, priceless Marbles, too big for the lift, taken down to Aldwych Station? They were taken on a low-loader truck – presumably slowly and on empty night roads – to Fulham in west London, where, at Lillie Road freight depot, they could be loaded on to a converted tube train to make their commute to Aldwych.

A DEARTH OF PASSENGERS

Less well known is Blake Hall Station on the Central Line, which closed because it had about six passengers a day, who all knew each other. Situated in open countryside, it was never going to be a hub. It was not even on mains electricity, but was fed by the Tube railway. Passengers fondly remembered the way lights dimmed as trains pulled in and out of the station, vying for power. It did hit the news in 1976, when a drought-crazed rabbit attacked a train driver through his open door.

Mayfair's Down Street also closed, in 1932, for lack of passengers. The locals were simply too posh to bother with Tube travel. Another casualty of posh opposition was North End in Hampstead. It was built but never opened, because residents were worried about the effect of trains on Hampstead Heath above. At 67.3m (221ft) deep, it is the deepest station on the Underground. The 197 steps down to it remain. With its great depth, it was used as a Cold War bunker.

At the other end of the social scale, the original Acton Town Station closed because it was on a little-used spur to South Acton, served by a train of just one carriage, known as 'the Ginny' to locals until closure in 1959. 'The Ginny' was a corruption of the Victorian locomotive called Jenny which used to ply the line.

WHITE CITY AND WOOD LANE

The original White City Station was built of wood, being a temporary stop for the 'Franco-British Exhibition' of 1908, held near Shepherd's Bush. It closed in 1914 and burnt down in 1959.

The original Wood Lane Station on the Central Line in west London was closed in 1947 and demolished in 2003. Bits of it are in the London Transport Museum, and this humble station near the old BBC Television Centre has cult status for two reasons. The classic *Dalek Invasion of the Earth* was filmed here in 1964, featuring the first Dr Who, William Hartnell. Secondly, it was the site of an engineering marvel, unique in the world – a piece of eccentricity so brave that it deserved to work, and it did.

The problem was a sharp curve in the track where two lines met. This made the platform gap dangerously wide for passengers mounting their train. The platform could not be rebuilt because of 'complex pointwork'. So a softwood (for lightness) moveable platform, 10.6m (35ft) long, was built. Controlled by a lever in a signal box, it moved 'electro-pneumatically' on rollers, about 120 times every day.

A VISION OF THE FUTURE?

In 1853, the historian Lord Macaulay poetically imagined, in the future, someone sketching the ruins of London from a broken arch of London Bridge. Perhaps these ghost stations hint of such a future, as evoked in the post-apocalyptic Thunderbirds episode called *Vault of Death* in which our plastic heroes explore a derelict Piccadilly Circus Station.

THE CONCRETE JUNGLE

✦ ✦ ✦

Seven obscure men in suits did more damage to London than the Luftwaffe. These were the leading British brutalist architects, who dotted London with cement monoliths. They were all inspired by one great notion, the radical German Bauhaus movement.

THE BAUHAUS

The leading light at the Bauhaus art school in 1920s Germany was an architect called Walter Gropius, a Berlin genius who married Mahler's widow. His one London house, in Chelsea Old Church Street, is a modern masterpiece which, unlike later brutalist homes, actually works for humans. It is like a long, low garden room and complements the old houses around it. But Gropius's eloquence, his talk of ending 'salon art' and of a 'machine economy' went to the heads of his followers. Art historian Ben Davis tracked down a surviving Bauhaus member, a German who called himself Tut. Tut recalled the Bauhaus as a 'dippy aesthetic commune' full of short-skirted girls and shaggy-haired theorists. Hitler was unsurprisingly unimpressed. He closed the Bauhaus school down in 1933.

Little did the Führer know that those 100 or so Bauhaus members would achieve, by inspiration, what the full might of his air force failed to do: the disruption of London's traditional skyline. The Bauhaus inspired the idea of concrete mass housing for the 'proletariat'. Old notions of beauty were sacrificed to the idea of a house as 'a machine for living in'. The most important practitioner of Bauhaus architecture was Henri Le Corbusier, whose dreadful grid-plan city in India I have stayed in.

BRUTALISM

The Bauhaus was revered for decades by the English chattering classes. Bauhaus was radical, it was obscure, and it lent god-like status to architects. In the 1950s and 1960s, it was the inspiration for a new architectural movement, brutalism. This produced some fine, well-functioning London buildings, but, in hundreds of cases, it caused the sort of fundamental misery depicted in J. G. Ballard's 1975 novel *High Rise*. In the novel, Ballard's arrogant architect ends up setting dogs on to the disgruntled residents of his London tower block.

Ballard's backlash against the high-rise was reinforced by Tom Wolfe's 1981 book *From Bauhaus to Our House*, which first revealed the baleful legacy of this brutal building style in cities. In the same vein, in 2009 Hal Foster, curator of the Museum of Modern Art's Bauhaus exhibition in New York, could write in his exhibition catalogue: 'Bauhaus committed the original sin of modernism, its naïve hunger for universals.'

The following seven 'unmagnificent men' were major
brutalist architects.

SIR BASIL SPENCE

Sir Basil Spence (1907–76) lived in a Tudor cottage in Yaxley,
Suffolk. Spence, a remorseless self-publicist with a Terry-Thomas
moustache, was a bounder. His disregard for context – and for
peasants – is shown in the lavish interiors and furniture he
designed for the viceroy's palace in New Delhi. After this, Spence
designed tower blocks for Glaswegians, which caused such misery
that they have been demolished.

It seems incredible that permission was granted for his brutal,
Orwellian Ministry of Justice (ex-Home Office) near St James's
Park. He insisted on 'geometric monumentality for London'.
His most notorious building is the high-rise tower block of the
cavalry barracks in Knightsbridge, which he justified in feverish
language: 'It is a muscular tower, not mimsy-pimsy. It's for
soldiers. On horses. In armour.' Sydenham council is battling to
demolish his Sydenham School and residents of his blocks of flats
in Feltham and Shepperton certainly have reason to regret Basil's
career choice.

JOHN BANCROFT

John Bancroft (1928–2011) lived in an old country cottage.
A London County Council architect, his low point was his
Pimlico Comprehensive School of 1964, a concrete block sunk
in a concrete rectangle, 'like a battleship'. Like much brutalist

architecture in London, it was technically incompetent. Clashing with its surroundings, the rain-streaked cement cracked and spalled. Pupils baked in summer but shivered in winter. There is a 2009 online interview of him at home, surrounded by antiques, saying how wonderfully the building works. The education authority Ofsted put the school on 'special measures' and Westminster council, wisely identifying brutalism as the problem, demolished it in 2010, in the teeth of a campaign by academics to preserve it.

RICHARD SEIFERT

Richard Seifert (1910–2001) lived in a walnut-panelled north London house with a 1.2-hectare (3-acre) garden. Seifert was a wheeler-dealer who dropped his Jewish first name, Rubin, and mysteriously styled himself Colonel Seifert. Driven everywhere in a Rolls, he was the first architect millionaire. Even a friendly obituary referred to his 'buccaneering activities' and 'impregnable self-righteousness'. He is the biggest offender of the seven, having cynically littered London with over 600 low-spec variations on a shoebox. His modus operandi was bending planning rules. His triumph was Centre Point (117m/ 385ft) high. Here he used legal

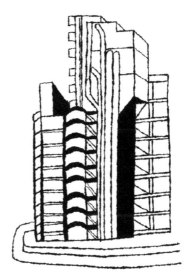

loopholes to break planning guidelines restricting height, and bribed the car-worshipping planners with a new roundabout. Centre Point, at the bottom of Tottenham Court Road, is both ugly and a white elephant, having no pavements. With its much-derided cost-cutting low ceilings, it has lain empty for much of its life.

Among his achievements, the Tolworth Tower has kept Tolworth a dangerous and deprived area, the Royal Garden Hotel looms over Kensington Palace (it made Princess Margaret cry), the King's Mall shopping centre turned Hammersmith into, well, anywhere, and the Hilton Hotel in Edgware Road and the Holborn Centre are soulless tracts in the centre of London. His NatWest Tower is the only building which Londoners might have thanked the IRA for bombing (fortunately casualty-free). After a long battle, in 2014, Network Rail got permission to demolish Seifert's gimcrack Euston Station.

JOHN POULSON

John Poulson (1910–93) lived in various Yorkshire mansions. Poulson was sentenced to seven years in jail for rigging planning decisions and bribing councillors. The judge called him 'incalculably evil' and even his defence QC called him 'self-righteous, and something of a megalomaniac'. His connections with Home Secretary Reggie Maudling led to Maudling's resignation but his concrete monuments remain: flats, offices and Cannon Street Station, **HIS CONCRETE MONUMENTS REMAIN: FLATS, OFFICES AND CANNON STREET STATION, WATERLOO STATION AND EAST CROYDON STATION, ALL OF WHICH HAVE WORSENED MONDAY MORNINGS FOR MILLIONS.**

Waterloo Station and East Croydon Station, all of which have worsened Monday mornings for millions. He was not even a properly trained architect. When his first employer heard that Poulson was setting up a practice he said, 'Christ, he couldn't design a brick shithouse.'

SIR FREDERICK GIBBERD

Sir Frederick Gibberd (1908–84) lived in a country house in Essex, which housed his large collection of paintings. Quietly prolific and consistently uninspired, this Coventry tailor's son wrote books on town design and was proudest of his Harlow New Town in Essex. He did damage in London with Arundel Great Court, a giant concrete block which erased three ancient streets between the Strand and the Thames, including the house where Tsar Peter the Great had lodged. Pevsner lamented its 'drab efficiency',[1] but at least this is only used as offices: people actually have to live in Gibberd's modernist estates in Streatham, Sydenham and Southgate.

PETER SMITHSON

Peter Smithson (1923–2003) spent many of his years in clean, orderly Bath. I think he was mad – a simplistic word which I do not use lightly. Luckily the BBC made an early documentary about Peter, who usually worked with his wife, fellow northerner Alison. The film was made by working-class Londoner and experimental artist, B. S. Johnson. Johnson is a cult figure, whose suicide in 1973 adds poignancy to the film. It shows the Smithsons as very creepy, either on drugs or high on their own theory.

Peter, who actually coined the term 'brutalism', and called himself Brutus at college, spawned the huge Robin Hood Gardens estate in Poplar, east London. On film, he happily compared the blocks to huge filing cabinets, and obsessed about their cleanliness: 'no need for grass cutting ... easy access from our streets-in-the-sky to mass transit systems'. He insisted that the 'stress-free' flats would 'release them and change them' (the workers, he meant).

The clue to the Smithsons' insanity is their clothing in the film. Alison wears a metallic spacesuit top with a pink Lurex tie and Peter is a futuristic spiv. Given a space at the Ideal Home Exhibtion, they made a space-age, super-clean habitat, filled with Aryan-style foil-clad inhabitants.

Sadly London's working class did not fit in with the Smithsons' ideal. Alison intoned robotically: 'The week it opened, they would shit in the lifts.' Asked why by a nervous interviewer, she said 'It's social jealousy ... London has never faced up to being more than a collection of villages' – i.e. Londoners should join a Smithson dream of mass living in a concrete utopia. In 2014, after years of crime and misery and despite a campaign by academics to get the Robin Hood flats listed, they were demolished.

If the Smithsons sound like Bond villains, our final brutalist actually was one ...

ERNÖ GOLDFINGER

Ernö Goldfinger (1902–87) had the decency to live in a modernist house, albeit in privileged Hampstead. Tall, striking Ernö, who grew up in Transylvania, was 'humourless and tense, explosive and uncompromising'. When he tried to sue Ian Fleming for making him a Bond villain, Fleming asked his publishers if they could put an erratum slip in every copy of *Goldfinger* to change his name to Goldprick.

Ernö was soaked in Bauhaus thought, having studied with Le Corbusier himself in Paris. Of his three brutalist 'masterpieces' in London, Trellick Tower in North Kensington is the most famous. This 30-storey tower of council flats never worked well from the start. I was there: I worked in the small library opposite Trellick Tower in 1974, two years after it was built. I was often terrified, for it was a war zone. People were raped on the often unlit stairwells, which had to be used because the lifts kept breaking down. The library was a refuge for fugitives from gang beatings and muggings. Yes, it was a tough area, but Trellick Tower was the hothouse of brutality. And it did not function as a 'machine for living in' either; it was usually either freezing or too hot inside. Trellick Tower now features in pop songs and is a Grade II listed building. The flats, protected by CCTV, guards and intercoms, are now sought-after private residences, but estimates to make Trellick Tower function thermally run into millions of pounds.

SUCCESS AND FAILURE

Despite the horrors above, the Bauhaus movement did spawn a few of London's best and most exciting buildings, like the Festival Hall (Leslie Martin), the National Theatre (Denys Lasdun) and the Commonwealth Institute (Robert Matthew), and good even came from the 'unmagnificent' seven featured above. The fight to save old buildings from their various schemes kick-started today's building conservation movement.

But brutalism had 'a flawed recognition of the human element', a 'mechanical view of human nature',[2] and it inflicted miseries which far outweighed its successes. A study of Sunni–Shia relations in Iraq found that the two opposing groups got on best in the old city of Basra because of the intricate medieval street plan, which depended on odd-shaped houses and encouraged continual human interaction. In new Basra and in Baghdad's brutalist boulevards, Sunni and Shia ghettoes war with each other.

Smithson was wrong. London works best as a series of villages.

Notes
1. Nikolaus Pevsner and Simon Bradley, *London, Volume 6, Westminster* (Yale University Press, London, 2003), p.370.
2. The words of ex-prison psychiatrist Theodore Dalrymple.

BOOKSHOPS AND BOOKSELLERS

✦ ✦ ✦

'Thank God! Cecil Court is still Cecil Court.' Happily, Graham Greene's words still hold good. The short, pedestrian-only street, a 'rookery' or slum until about 1910, links Charing Cross Road and St Martin's Lane. It is still full of the small, specialist bookshops that Greene loved. The best time to visit is on a winter afternoon, preferably in the rain. The Salisbury pub adds atmosphere, with a pure 1892 interior much used in films and so

THE BEST TIME TO VISIT IS ON A WINTER AFTERNOON, PREFERABLY IN THE RAIN.

atmospheric that Peter O'Toole, filming overseas, had a contract clause that he would be flown back regularly to drink there. He once bought everybody there a drink; he'd just landed the part of Lawrence of Arabia. Enjoyable temporal vertigo: Lawrence himself bought books in Cecil Court.

John Le Carré's spymaster Smiley shopped here and Smiley-esque figures still people Cecil Court. The atmosphere, the steamed-up windows, the fact you have to press a bell to get in some shops, the plaque where Mozart lived – all give a timeless European atmosphere of scholarly intrigue (see box). In 1772, Robert Dixon at Number 10 sold Masonic books. Only in Cecil Court could you sell the secrets of a secret fraternity. In 1790, an atheist debating club met in Cecil Court until a police raid. In 1938 the Franco regime threatened the family of Catalan Joan Gili, who ran the Republican bookshop at Number 5, a hub for anti-fascists (now it's the Italian Bookshop). In a 1950 photograph of Number 8, bookseller Bob Chris sits near a neat sign over the fireplace: 'Do not mistake courtesy on my part as an invitation to stay all day'.

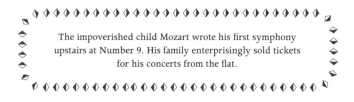

The impoverished child Mozart wrote his first symphony upstairs at Number 9. His family enterprisingly sold tickets for his concerts from the flat.

WATKINS BOOKS

Number 19 is the still-vibrant occult specialist Watkins Books (est. 1893), which incidentally sells more books on world religions than any shop in the world. John Watkins, the founder, was a friend of Madame Blavatsky, a Russian who had known Tolstoy. Blavatsky, who held famous seances, met a being in Hyde Park she called 'The Teacher', and wrote the monumental *Secret Doctrine*. Some see her as a pioneer Tibetologist and prophet of nuclear fission. To others, she is a table-rapping bullshitter.

When I went there in 2014, astrology readings were taking place behind velvet curtains in the window. I went downstairs. Discussing the basement's history with a bookseller and how in the 1930s Aleister Crowley conducted occult ceremonies there which Yeats attended, he said 'Yes, the shop is a meme': you only get these comments (which I do not understand) in bookshops.

MARCHPANE

Crossing the Yorkstone paving, I rang the bell of Number 16, Marchpane, a children's bookshop like Flourish and Blotts in Diagon Alley: appropriately, I see a first edition of *Harry Potter* inside. The pleasing disorder makes me think of an Agatha Christie line about a bookshop: 'The books owned the shop, not the other way about. They had run wild.'[1] The proprietor sits up in a sort of pulpit amid piles of books and ephemera, towers and valleys of stories. Many books I look at cost hundreds, but I buy an Enid Blyton illustration from a cardboard box for £20. As I pay, I notice for the first time that there is a full-sized original dalek in the middle of the floor.

FOYLES

Cecil Court bookseller Dick Hartwell recalled, in 1931, 'a rough-looking tramp with ankle-length coat' coming in. About to give him a few bob, he was told: 'That's Willie Foyle!' Foyles opened first at Number 16 Cecil Court in 1903, before moving to Charing Cross Road.

THE RICH HISTORY OF FOYLES BOOKSHOP INCLUDES SENDING AN OVERDUE NOTICE TO THE POPE, AND WRITING TO HITLER TO STOP HIM BURNING BOOKS.

The rich history of Foyles bookshop includes sending an overdue notice to the Pope, and writing to Hitler to stop him burning books. Christina Foyle suggested he send them to her instead. The Führer replied, refusing on the grounds that he did not want to corrupt Londoners. Foyles is now very smart, but in the old days – about the time I was unsuccessfully interviewed by Christina – I saw an untidy mound of books next to an escalator. Above it, a felt-tip sign with an arrow pointing down read 'Don't look here'. A policeman once saw a customer inside in the small hours, pounding on the window; engrossed in Dostoyevsky, he had been locked in.

RUNNERS AND LOVERS

Sir Robert Sherston-Baker, who still runs a Canterbury bookshop, was a new boy in 1973 at Sawyer's bookshop off Charing Cross Road. He thought his first job would be to chuck out a tramp whose coat was tied with string but no, said Mr Sawyer, this was Mr Howlett, one of London's best 'runners'. Runners bought bargains for resale – early eBay.[2]

Another unlikely bookshop character could be encountered in Hampstead in 1934, at Booklovers' Corner. A tall, 'De Gaulle-like' assistant stood forbiddingly in the shop. George Orwell never sat down, and did not generally like customers, except for a girl called Kay Ekevall. His *Burmese Days* and *Down and out in Paris and London* had already come out. They chatted about Swift, and became lovers. Novelist Russell Hoban also found love in a bookshop, Truslove and Hanson, conducting after-hours, shop-floor trysts with fellow bookseller Gundula Ahl, who became his second wife (see box). Bookshops can be aphrodisiac; Pepys kept returning to one in Duck Lane to kiss the owner's wife.

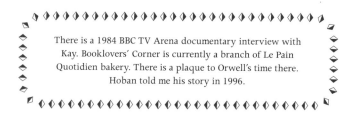

There is a 1984 BBC TV Arena documentary interview with Kay. Booklovers' Corner is currently a branch of Le Pain Quotidien bakery. There is a plaque to Orwell's time there. Hoban told me his story in 1996.

WATERSTONES

London bookselling was transformed in the late twentieth century by Tim Waterstone. This Cambridge-educated son of a Calcutta tea broker had a lifelong passion for books and a maverick streak. Sacked from W. H. Smith's books division – some say because he loved books too much – he set up his own shop in Old Brompton Road in 1982. He never planned to make it a chain, but Londoners loved the idea of a late-opening, well-stocked bookshop, staffed by intelligent enthusiasts. Warm red carpets and black shelving were lit by spotlights sourced by the first Mrs Waterstone (see box).

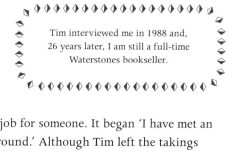

Tim interviewed me in 1988 and, 26 years later, I am still a full-time Waterstones bookseller.

Tim Waterstone was a kind man. Working at the Kensington shop, I remember a memo from him, asking us to find a job for someone. It began 'I have met an Algerian on the Underground.' Although Tim left the takings in a carrier bag on the Tube just before that first Christmas in 1982, his bookshops were so successful that his old employer W. H. Smith paid him a large sum for the chain, which is still going, under Russian ownership. Thousands of authors' events in Waterstones brought readers and writers closer together. These could be Rabelaisian occasions: tramps in the doorway of the Charing Cross Road branch of Waterstones banged on the window in protest at a noisy book launch: they could not get to sleep.

It is a measure of Tim Waterstone's eccentric integrity that, asked in a survey for his favourite bookshop while he was running Waterstones, he said 'Foyles.'

SMALL BOOKSHOPS

Conversely, when Nancy Mitford was a wartime bookseller at the still-thriving Heywood Hill Bookshop in Mayfair, she forgot to lock up altogether. The next morning she recalled, 'I saw lots of customers trying to sell books to each other.'

These smaller bookshops are a glory of London: John Sandoe in the backstreets of Chelsea, with its bookcases which slide out of the wall; Daunt Books of Marylebone; the Arabic bookshop Al Saqi in Notting Hill, founded by female Lebanese peace activist Mai Ghoussoub in 1979 and still going strong. Maggs Bros. in Berkeley Square (est. 1853) is still run by a Mr Maggs, where staff within living memory wore tails, and you can buy Maggs's book oil for leather bindings. Henry Sotheran's off Piccadilly is going strong too. The oldest antiquarian booksellers in the world, they bought the library of Laurence Sterne and sold their one-off, jewel encrusted *Rubaiyat of Omar Khayyam* to an American who went down on the *Titanic*, with the book.

SLANEY AND MCKAY

In the 1980s, until a rent hike closed it, Slaney and McKay was a distinctive small bookshop. Set up by Sally Slaney and Lesley McKay after they both got divorced, it sold new books from the ground floor and basement of a Chelsea house. A shop cat lounged on second-hand furniture, but always leapt into action to attack Manolo Blahnik's tiny dog. There was no air-conditioning, but a large Victorian window was often open, curtains flapping, letting river breezes into the children's section.

Art and drama were specialities, and Ruth Hadden, a Liverpudlian who trained at Collet's socialist bookshop in Charing Cross Road, ran a 'Style and Gender' section beloved of punks and the young. No marketing expert would have attempted to target both Italian fans of The Cure and Chelsea's arty elite, but somehow it worked and I was lucky to be the manager.

I treasure a letter from a regular, Elisabeth Collins, calling the shop 'a place of light'. Collins often came in with her famous bearded husband, Cecil Collins, whose 'Fool' paintings adorned the Tate. As an obituarist said, 'He had great physical calm, with long, thin fingers with which he would seemingly shape his sentences as he spoke.' I wish I had known then that the always friendly Elisabeth, tall and elegant with big hats and flowing scarves, was not only 'the muse' but a Chagall-like genius herself, who first painted the clown image which became her husband's leitmotif. The Tate has now snapped up four of her rare paintings. What a household they had around the corner in Paultons Square, a home shared for 30 years with Gavin Maxwell's muse, the poet Kathleen Raine, she who called his Scottish home the 'Ring of Bright Water'.

Slaney and McKay was like any bookshop in being a place to slow down and sort a few things out, but it had some exceptional regulars, who connected with each other. Francis Bacon bought art books. Brian Eno bought music books. Charlie Watts ordered obscure military history and Mickey Rourke bought Stephen King novels.

A tearful Michael Hordern, newly widowed, bought Delia Smith's *One is Fun!* with the words 'It's not, y'know.' Hordern's long-running affair with the actress Coral Browne lends piquancy to those tears (see box). Later, I told Hordern that Anthony Hopkins had been in, puzzling in the psychology section over Lear, whom he was about to play. On Hopkins's next visit I conveyed the advice of Hordern, whose notable Lear was sadly never filmed: 'Tell him you can't do Lear without a sense of humour.'

Alan J. Lerner, who wrote musicals such as *My Fair Lady*, often asked why I had no book on musicals. Curiously, there wasn't one, but just before he died, Lerner wrote one.

For some reason, the weather outside defines the bookshop experience inside. To me it was always summer in Slaney and McKay, with the window open and a soundscape of traffic, talking passers-by, birdsong in the square opposite and the beep of the pedestrian crossing outside. I was a divorcee, like the shop's owners, and my daughter Ailsa often pottered around the kids' section, where the most lively regulars were the Geldof children.

THE WEATHER OUTSIDE DEFINES THE BOOKSHOP EXPERIENCE INSIDE. TO ME IT WAS ALWAYS SUMMER IN SLANEY AND MCKAY.

NURTURING AND CAMPAIGNING

London bookshops have historically sponsored new literature. Different booksellers paid £5,000 to publish Pope's translation of Homer, £200 for Jonathan Swift's *Gulliver's Travels*, and £5 for John Milton's *Paradise Lost* (apparently a turkey). When a customer asked to buy Milton's masterpiece, the bookseller said 'Buy it all sir, I am using it as kindling and I hear he has a sequel.' It was Dodsley, a bookseller, who suggested to Samuel Johnson that he write a dictionary, and another bookseller was responsible for Boswell meeting Johnson.

The shops have also been radical campaign centres. John Hatchard (1768–1849) founded Hatchard's in Piccadilly. This good-hearted fellow, who always wore a black frock coat 'like a bishop', ran a bookshop/coffee shop with a crackling fireplace. Snores often came from the leather armchairs. Hatchard's support for the anti-slavery campaign significantly contributed to its success. In modern times, Gay's the Word bookshop has campaigned for gay rights for 30 years, despite being raided by police and suffering a firebomb attack. Compendium (closed in 2001) in Camden High Street was the leading alternative bookshop, full of imports and radical philosophy. It says a lot for its pulling power and nonchalant attitude to marketing that nobody attended an event with Baudrillard, the French philosopher who inspired *The Matrix*. The Clash wrote a song about Compendium.

Most of all, London bookshops provide an opportunity for serendipity, for finding a book you never knew existed, for unlocking a new part of your soul. This is why the author of *84 Charing Cross Road*, Helene Hanff, wrote: 'Standing there looking at the shelves crammed with books, I felt myself relax and was suddenly at peace.'

Notes
1. *The Clocks* (Collins, 1963).
2. Sheila Markham, *A Book of Booksellers* (Oak Knoll Press, 2007).

FOUR SHOPS, FOUR WOMEN

✦ ✦ ✦

George Devine (1910–66) was the son of a Hendon bank clerk. A retiring figure in his lifetime, he is virtually unknown now, but he helped to start a revolution in London culture, an outburst of creativity comparable with Elizabethan times. This big man, who wore black-rimmed glasses, chunky jumpers and smoked a pipe, was decorated for wartime bravery in Burma. Getting into acting at Oxford, he soon learned that he was not matinee-idol material, and became the artistic director of the Royal Court Theatre in Sloane Square.

When Devine read John Osborne's *Look Back in Anger* in 1955, a sulphurous play about a working-class man and his dysfunctional marriage, he knew he had to stage it. Osborne had no phone so Devine rowed himself out to the playwright's Thames houseboat at Battersea. Osborne was in, and delighted. The play, and the Richard Burton film, had a witty impatience with class-ridden wartime attitudes. Its influence, in Mary Quant's words, 'spilled out on to the streets of London'.

MARY QUANT: BAZAAR

Also in 1955, Quant, a Blackheath-born fashion designer with a bewitching Welsh energy — she was of mining descent — opened a shop called Bazaar in Chelsea's King's Road, on the corner of Markham Square. Osborne came in, and so did Audrey Hepburn and Brigitte Bardot, because Bazaar was revolutionary.

Quant, who never went to fashion school, had started on £3 a week in the back room of a Mayfair hat shop. In Bazaar she used her pattern-cutting skills and the results of magpie-like raids on old-fashioned Soho haberdasheries. She adapted tab-collar men's shirts for women and used tweeds, jerseys and new dress and blouse shapes to change the face of fashion. A French fashion historian has classed her with Dior and Chanel in a holy trinity. At night, she would change her windows: Londoners flocked to see each new display.

> WHEN SHE PIONEERED THE MINISKIRT, BOWLER-HATTED MEN BANGED ON HER WINDOW AND SHOUTED 'IMMORAL!', 'DISGUSTING!' ... LATER, SHE CAME UP WITH HOT PANTS, WHICH MUST HAVE DRIVEN THE BOWLER-HATTED MEN TO EARLY GRAVES.

When she pioneered the miniskirt, bowler-hatted men banged on her window and shouted 'Immoral!', 'Disgusting!' Miniskirts were too short for stockings, so Quant got women into tights: the only place she could source them was a theatrical costumier's in St Martin's Lane. Later, she came up with hot pants, which must have driven the bowler-hatted men to early graves. All this was in a Chelsea she remembers as 'shabby and charming, more like Paris than London. Locals went out in dressing gown and slippers to buy their morning bread at Mrs Beaton's the baker.'[1]

BARBARA HULANICKI: BIBA

The next small shop to change London opened in 1964, over the road from the house I grew up in. At that time, Scarsdale Villas, off Earl's Court Road, was more downbeat than now – our house contained, as well as my parents, my seven siblings, an Irish family, an actress, and a retired female spy.

Over the road was a chemist's shop, with large, pear-shaped blue glass jars in the window. Barbara Hulanicki, a Pole, bought the shop, left the glass jars in place and called the shop 'Biba'. As a 9-year-old I peered in with wonder: loud music, dark, Art Nouveau flock wallpaper and girls of impossible coolness. Hulanicki had studied at Brighton Art College – now the University of Brighton – and her shop was chic, decadent and friendly. Crowds gathered outside as Biba repeatedly sold out of trademark items such as the brown pinstripe dress.

When, in 1974, the shop moved to take over the Derry and Toms department store in Kensington High Street, it became a black and gold Aladdin's cave. I remember the amazing feeling of being able to just sit about on comfy sofas; no officious assistants moved you on. The new Biba sold clothes but also in black and gold, art nouveau tins, paint and baked beans. It even sold black terry nappies. It had a children's floor and a bookshop. On the top floor was a rock venue, but if you pressed 'R' in the lift it opened on a rural scene: a roof garden, with trees, ponds and flamingos. The roof garden remains. A new generation of creative Londoners came here for inspiration: David Bowie, Mick Jagger, Twiggy, and an unknown called Freddie Mercury, who sold second-hand clothes in nearby Kensington Market. Mercury took taxis a lot, because he knew he was going to be famous one day.

Despite these celebrities, Biba clothes were incredibly cheap. Typically, a dress was £3. Hulanicki wanted interesting clothes to be affordable, not confined to the catwalk. After she closed Biba – since the Zionist assassination of her diplomat father in Jerusalem she regarded everything as fleeting – women in the street tearfully begged her to reopen.

LEE BENDER: BUS STOP

At the same time in 1969 young Lee Bender, who studied at St Martin's School of Art, opened Bus Stop, just by the Number 27 bus stop in Kensington Church Street. The Race Relations Act had just been passed and Bender made a point of employing black and white staff – revolutionary in Kensington then. Midway between the deprived black population of Notting Hill and white Kensington High Street, she catered for both with radical fashion, building on the fearlessness and fun of Quant and Hulanicki. Customers included Lauren Bacall. Melvyn Bragg has said that Bus Stop typified the way a shop can mould a whole generation.[2]

VIVIENNE WESTWOOD: SEX

Meanwhile, another young girl was flunking out of Harrow Art School's fashion course after only a year, to be a primary school teacher. As Vivienne Westwood reflected later: 'I just didn't see how a working-class girl like me could make a career in the art world.' She started running a Saturday jewellery stall in Portobello Market, the tatty part under the flyover. (Today, it is still the most bohemian and interesting part of the market.)

After becoming the girlfriend of Malcolm McLaren, the Sex Pistols' manager, Westwood left teaching in 1971 to open a shop at 140 Kings Road, near Chelsea Town Hall. After various name changes, it became 'SEX'. Westwood blended heavy metal biker outfits and sadomasochistic gear to create punk fashion. She was a cultural revolutionary and 'the godmother of punk'.

I ran a bookshop on King's Road and on the broad pavement outside SEX, I watched bikers on Harley Davidsons mingle with punks in Mohican haircuts, sneering and spitting. ('Punk' is an old London word for a disruptive ruffian.) People came to parade in King's Road from all over the world. As McLaren said, rock was a jungle beat that threatened Western civilization: punk attacked it head-on. The art school musicians of punk were enacting unexplained spectacles to challenge the sleepwalking passers-by. This 'situationism' came from Guy Debord, the Svengali behind the 1968 Paris riots. Debord came to London once, to talk at the Institute of Contemporary Arts in the Mall in 1960. After a short time, he told the adoring audience of jumper-wearing beatniks they were 'stupid c***s' and left. He shot himself in 1994.

Like her friend and fellow Londoner Katherine Hamnett, Vivienne Westwood still uses her fashion shows to campaign on social issues, from nuclear disarmament to the meat industry. This hell-raising art school dropout is now Dame Vivienne Westwood. Like Quant, Bender and Hulanicki, her clothes are in museums but she has carried on designing. Their four shops have no plaques, but they changed history.

Notes

1. Mary Quant, *Autobiography* (Headline, 2012), p.25. Also used: Barbara Hulanicki, *From A to Biba* (Victoria and Albert Museum, 2007), Barbara Hulanicki on *Desert Island Discs* (BBC Radio 4). Lee Bender, *Bus Stop and the Influence of the 70s on Fashion Today* (A & C Black, 2010) and Andrew Hussey, *The Game of War: The Life and Death of Guy Debord* (Jonathan Cape, 2001).
2. Conversation with the author, 1988.

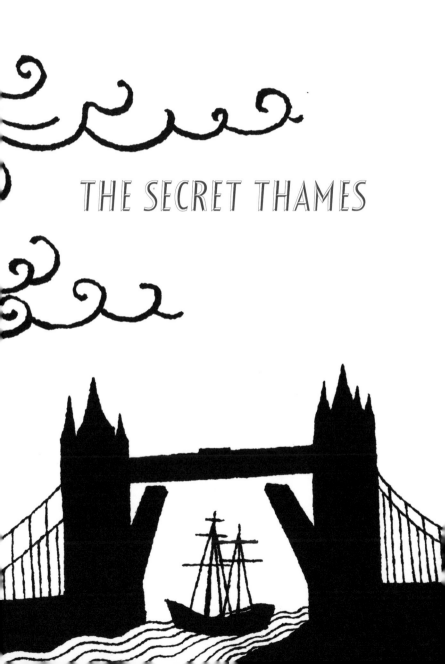

THE SECRET THAMES

SECRET STREAMS

✦ ✦ ✦

'T hat bastard priest', my father used to say in the 1960s, with the humorous relish of a character in a Harold Pinter play. He was referring to Father Dain, the Catholic prelate of Our Lady of Victories, Kensington, who failed to return my Dad's copy of *The Lost Rivers of London* by Nicholas Barton. He still has the book, so, if a geriatric Father Dain is reading this I say again: 'Bastard!'

This rarely seen book by an eccentric hand surgeon, written in 1962 and published by Leicester University Press, is the Dead Sea scrolls of the waters under London. It is a palimpsest of oral testimony, cartographic detective work, archival research and the plodding around London which, the author insisted, is the only way to rediscover London's hidden watercourses (see box).

> Palimpsest: analogically, a text comprised of multiple different forms of text.

LESLIE LATHAM, DOWSER

My father, Leslie Latham, arrived at his interest in underground water by a strange route: his life was a Dickensian tale. In 1913 he was born out of wedlock in St Pancras workhouse, his father a visiting sailor. A few months later, his mother abandoned him and he was adopted by a Bethnal Green policeman and his wife. My father always said that he was left on the street in fish-and-chip paper, and that Fred the policeman picked him up. The East End then, twenty years after Jack the Ripper, was a dangerous place but Fred was widely respected: he was the only copper who could patrol alone rather than with a colleague.

> HIS MOTHER ABANDONED HIM AND HE WAS ADOPTED BY A BETHNAL GREEN POLICEMAN AND HIS WIFE. MY FATHER ALWAYS SAID THAT HE WAS LEFT ON THE STREET IN FISH-AND-CHIP PAPER, AND THAT FRED THE POLICEMAN PICKED HIM UP.

Leslie left school at 14, becoming in turn a gardener, gravedigger, plumber's mate and then, from 1933, a private in the army. It was in the army that he began a strange, lifelong relationship with hidden watercourses: he learned to dowse. A dowser finds water using a rod; the apparently magical rod simply amplifies muscular changes that occur in all of us over water. Bushmen in the Kalahari Desert can still dowse by simply stretching out their hands. Anyway, the army had a surprising number of dowsers, who simply viewed this odd talent as a country craft like thatching or drystone walling.

DISCOVERING BUILDINGS

Dowsers can detect the lack of water as well, so lines of masonry, drier than the surrounding earth, can be dowsed. In 1938, when Latham was stationed at Kensington barracks in Kensington Church Street (see box), he dowsed the existence of a Roman villa under the barrack square. Understandably, the commanding officer was unwilling to dig up this area, the scene of daily square-bashing. But one day after a light fall of snow, my father persuaded his CO to accompany him to the roof of nearby St Mary Abbots Church. With the snow differentially melted by the Roman grid-plan of stonework below, the villa's layout was clearly visible. The subsequent dig was featured in the Corps' journal and *The Observer*.

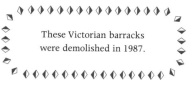

These Victorian barracks were demolished in 1987.

Latham's next discovery was a Tudor culvert, or water tunnel, from Kensington Palace to Chelsea Place (now Chelsea Royal Hospital). Henry VIII commissioned the building of this tunnel to deliver good spring water to his riverside residence.[1] Most of it has collapsed now, but it was traced heading in the right direction, south towards Chelsea. The conduit house at the head of the spring, though altered by Victorianism, can still be glimpsed in the back garden of one of the embassies overlooking Kensington Palace. My father could not investigate it in the 1930s because the millionaire who then occupied the house allegedly kept a lunatic daughter locked up in there, an unfortunate real-life version of the madwoman in the attic from *Jane Eyre*. Dad gleaned all such information from local pubs, the haunts of his wide circle of chums – the servants, coppers and undertakers of Kensington at the time.

FAME AND REWARDS

The tale of the cockney dowser – although my dad often affected an extraordinary fake posh accent which was almost parodic – attracted attention from the *Daily Mail*, which ran a profile of him with a picture of his 'book-lined study in Kensington', and from Queen Victoria's last daughter, Princess Louise, who summoned him to an audience in Kensington Palace. Latham went on to feature on BBC TV, and to dowse all sorts of water, including a well on Jersey for Gerald '*My Family and Other Animals*' Durrell. Superstitiously, he never accepted money for finding water, for fear that this would 'bugger up' his natural abilities.

THE TALE OF THE COCKNEY DOWSER - ALTHOUGH MY DAD OFTEN AFFECTED AN EXTRAORDINARY FAKE POSH ACCENT WHICH WAS ALMOST PARODIC - ATTRACTED ATTENTION FROM THE *DAILY MAIL*,

Latham had eight children – I am the seventh – and one day in the 1970s we received several crates of Britvic juices. Britvic, now a huge multinational, were then making juices at their old Docklands site in Beckton, a place so superbly desolate that *1984* was filmed there. Britvic, fed up with fluoridated tap water, wanted to use their original spring. They knew it was somewhere under the large tarmac loading yard, but not the exact location. My father dowsed it easily – by tapping his foot he could even break the signal and tell the depth of the spring – and Britvic, unable to pay him, sent the crates. The factory is still there.

Even better than the juices were the boxes of Penguin bars that BP sent after Latham located a lost pipe-cleaning 'pig' for them at the Canvey Island refinery. I went on that job and was amazed at the brisk certainty of his dowsing. The one proviso he gave to clients was that the area be cleared of tittering sceptics. When he was asked to dowse Westminster Abbey he uttered the same proviso and, although it was All Souls' Day, the dean closed the abbey completely for him to work in peace.

INHERITED SKILLS

I wish I could dowse, but I think too much. To be accurate, the dowser has to silence any mental suggestion and, in Francis Bacon's phrase about painting, 'unlock the valves of feeling'. There was, however, one among the eight children who could dowse. Paul Latham, now a successful architect, was also the most practical of the children. He accurately dowsed an underground stream in the back garden of our house, 49 Scarsdale Villas, behind Kensington High Street. Unfortunately it was in the middle of the lawn, so Paul made a turf cover for it with a metal lid. He then attached a tin to a rod (the tin having a valve in its base) so that we could lower it down the 1.2m (4ft) shaft to the stream and watch it fill with clear water, which tasted wonderful.

The stream added to the magic of that garden, where we sailed boats on a canal my father made, and I played Robin Hood endlessly amongst the unidentifiable exotic plants that sprang up from the elephant manure which Colonel Hudson, a big game hunter who lived next door, gave us.

After Hudson died Mr Henry, a retired signalman, moved in. Eager to re-create his past and permanently at war with his wife, he turned his first floor into private quarters, a pseudo-signal box. He even built an outside wooden staircase, of signal box pattern, so that he could come and go without seeing the wife.

LONDON CLAY

That underground stream ran over the London Clay Formation, a beautifully blue-grey geological deposit that sits in the huge bowl of chalk under London. The city is both on and of the clay, out of which London stock bricks were made. The lip of that deep bowl is visible as chalk near the surface in Croydon and Gravesend. At White's, a gentleman's club near St James's Palace, some Victorian chaps with plenty of time on their hands bored under the cellar and went through 71.6m (235ft) of clay before hitting the chalk.

Londoners have harnessed other clay streams. In 1845, a 91.4m-deep (300ft) spring behind the National Gallery, under Orange Street, was identified as vigorous enough to supply the fountains in the newly laid-out Trafalgar Square. The fountains, incidentally, had a secondary purpose of preventing large, rebellious assemblies. With the aid of a steam pump, the spring supplied the fountains until 1935, when the mains took over.

And behind the high, windowless, burglar-proof walls of the Bank of England there is a little-known garden with a fountain that used to shoot up 6m (20ft) into the air, making two old lime trees nearby sparkle. It was fed, until the twentieth century, by a

nearby stream, 100m (330ft) deep. In a marvel of engineering, the same steam engine that pumped the water also ran the banknote printing presses. The tinkling fountain had a strange companion from 1798 until 1933, and his story is irresistible.

Daniel Jenkins was a 2.1m (7ft) tall bank clerk who, during his terminal illness – he died at 31 – worried continually that his corpse would be stolen by bodysnatchers, who would be able to get £200 by selling him to surgeons for research. Jenkins's colleagues petitioned the Bank's governor about his plight and he was allowed to be buried by the fountain, 'safe as the Bank of England'. Fortunately, the bank's garden is consecrated ground, the site of a long-lost City church. In 1933 builders rediscovered the coffin and Jenkins was reburied in a Peckham cemetery for tedious legal reasons.

Although most of these watercourses on the clay are hidden, in the Middle Ages many were visible above ground. In 1174 William Fitzstephen's *Description of London* included: 'springs wholesome and clear, which ripple amid pebbles bright'. A characteristic noise of London then was the gentle clack of water mills.

TIRELESS WORKHORSES

London's rivers have been abused as storm-relief sewers, piped, diverted, plunged into darkness and ignored, but they still quietly perform their cosmic purpose of draining the hills into the Thames and the sea. They did this before London existed;

they may do it after London has crumbled. Before you imagine the previous sentence, try this Thomas Macaulay scene: he wrote that the Catholic Church will still be going strong when an artist from New Zealand, sitting on a broken arch of London Bridge, is sketching the ruins of London 'in a vast solitude'.[2]

THE RIVER FLEET

From prehistoric times right up until a few centuries ago, the two biggest rivers that ran through the central London area and into the Thames from the north were the Walbrook and the Fleet. Now, they have almost entirely disappeared from view.

The Fleet, which has its source in Hampstead and joins the Thames just south-west of St Paul's Cathedral, gave London its 'main harbourage', as Fitzstephen put it. It was big enough then to be navigated by the barges carrying stone to build the medieval St Paul's Cathedral. To the fury of many Londoners, Sir Christopher Wren spent a mind-boggling £74,000 on dredging the mouth of the Fleet and erecting a high-arching, Venetian-style bridge over the cleared-out, 15.2m-wide (50ft) tributary. From this era dates an anchor, found at Kentish Town. In 1800 an 80-year-old man reminisced about being ill as a boy in a house on Lamb's Conduit Street by the Fleet: the river ran under his window and a snipe whirred up from it one morning.

Although there is a charming picture of boys swimming in the River Fleet in 1815 at St Pancras, by 1850 it had been built over and renamed the Fleet sewer. Travel writer Eric Newby managed to see the Fleet at Blackfriars in 1974 on a trip with a sewer maintenance gang: 'It raced riverwards at a good ten knots, too strong to stand up in, down a 14-foot-high tunnel.' Mysteriously, an iron bedstead had recently come down it. You can still see the river rushing by, 6m (20ft) below a grating outside the Coach and Horses pub in Clerkenwell, and the cityscape still bears the imprint of this hidden river. Farringdon Street, wide and low, marks the lower Fleet valley. Holborn Viaduct sails high above it – its full name, Holborn Valley Viaduct, is still visible on its Victorian inscription.

YOU CAN STILL SEE THE RIVER RUSHING BY, 6M (20FT) BELOW A GRATING OUTSIDE THE COACH AND HORSES PUB IN CLERKENWELL.

THE TYBURN AND THE WESTBOURNE

The West End's river is the Tyburn, and Nicholas Barton gives tantalizing glimpses of it: in wartime his parents saw it running in a deep bomb crater; he prints a blurred 1957 picture of it running through roadworks; and an old lady told him that her Edwardian parents used to take her to hear it bubbling under Mayfair's Lansdowne Passage. More obviously, fashionable Marylebone Lane sinuously follows the Tyburn below, cutting across the surrounding grid-plan streets on its sweet way.

West London's big river, the Westbourne, is a little more visible. If you stand on Sloane Square Tube station and look up, you can see the huge pipe that carries the River Westbourne to its Thames outfall at Chelsea. On its way it passes old houses in Pimlico built on wooden platforms instead of proper foundations, because of the river. Upstream, the Westbourne is seen magnificently as it becomes the Serpentine in Kensington Gardens.

RIVERS OF SOUTH LONDON

South London has two great tributaries. Brixton's River Effra was a real flooder in its lower reaches. The flood area could never be built on, so it became a big cricket ground – The Oval. Wandsworth is named after the other great southern river, the Wandle. It has been cleaned up and the brown trout it was famous for in the seventeenth century are being reintroduced. The Victorian bore Ruskin might recognize its 'cress-set rivulets where sand danced and minnows darted'.

UNDISCOVERED WATERCOURSES

There is one mystery river that defeated even Barton's detective skills. In 1960, the owner of a Soho jazz club, the Mandrake, showed Barton, under a grating in the basement, a river strongly flowing southwards. Barton is dead and I cannot trace which house was the Mandrake in Meard Street. I hope this river is still running and perhaps, as Barton hints, it fed the water shows (sea battles, mermaid pageants and so on) that wowed Edwardian audiences at the Hippodrome Theatre (now a naff casino).

My father died long ago but I have his divining rod, in a cedar box he had made in the Aleppo souk during the war. It is made of two thin whalebone strips (from a woman's corset) whipped together at one end. I really must give it to Paul, and maybe he can find another of London's lost watercourses.

Notes
3. F. Sheppard, *Survey of London, Volume 37* (English Heritage, 1973) pp.162–93.
4. Thomas Babington Macaulay, reviewing Leopold Ranke's *Eccelesiastical and Political History of the Popes of Rome during the Sixteenth and Seventeenth Century* (3 vols., 1840) in the *Edinburgh Review* (1842).

A MYSTIC RIVER

✦ ✦ ✦

Sweet Thames, run softly, 'til I end my song.
Edmund Spenser, 1596

The Thames is a mystic river. It was in the old days and it is now, because river lore lives in all of us. That lore goes back too far and spreads too widely around the globe not to linger in our souls. The river is healer and nemesis; it gives life and death. We sense this still, 'at the heart's core' in Yeats's words, but cannot articulate it: every reader of this book has thrown a coin in a well as an offering to something. 'I cannot get away from it,' wrote Hilaire Belloc, 'that the Thames may be alive.'

I was on a night train entering Delhi when, at about 4am, we rumbled on to the iron Jamuna Bridge. A suited businessman went out on the platform between two carriages and uttered mantras to the sacred river. Rivers are, literally, awesome, although our Thames may look tamed. No wonder Alexander the Great did not stay long in India after he crossed the mighty Indus. For centuries, the Thames remained a border between tribes in ancient Britain.

APPEASING THE RIVER

River crossings require caution. From the dawn of time, rivers have been both deities and the abode of fickle spirits, who must be propitiated at fords. To the Hittites (about 1500 BC), the Tigris was such a personality that he made a goddess pregnant. Jacob in the Old Testament, whose noisy entourage woke up a river sprite, had to wrestle him all night. The King of the Spartans prevented this sort of tiring opposition by slaughtering a bull before he crossed the Erasinus, in which four spirits lived, including Pan himself. The macho Persian king Xerxes killed three white horses and 'performed other strange ceremonies' before a crossing, and the battle-hardened Roman general Lucullus killed a bull before crossing the Euphrates in Iraq.

Peruvians and the Bantu of Africa were less wealthy: they prayed and threw corn in the water before crossing. The Welsh were yet more frugal: they spat three times before crossing. The Masai throw grass, which is their treasure. The Baganda of Uganda used to give the river beer, and deemed it impertinent to rescue a man who lost his footing and got taken downriver.

In 1861, before the explorer John Speke could cross the Upper Nile, the 'resident wizard' killed two goats. Tamils in India throw a rupee in a ford, while their neighbours the Toda people cross with right arm outside their cloak as a mark of respect. In Indonesia, sins are quietly confessed during a crossing, whilst gypsies in Transylvania used to throw a puppet called Green George in the river.

Late in life, Xerxes lost his temper when the river swept his bridge away. He made his men give the waters 300 lashes, a peevishness worthy of the Papua New Guineans who fired arrows at an unruly river 'for hours'.[1]

WASHING SIN AWAY

Witches were usually burned but a particularly virulent one, who made effigies of men, voodoo-style, had to be drowned at London Bridge in 984. Swedish witches had to be drowned in holy water. In the same way, at Execution Dock in Wapping, until 1800, executed pirates were hung in the river until three tides had washed them. Until 1750 a ducking stool was in use at Kingston Bridge, immersing miscreants in cleansing water.

In the words of Jon Cotton, senior curator at the Museum of London, the Thames 'was seen as a sacred river, like the Ganges in India'.[2] We know that offerings abound in the river, as weapons have been found which are too unused and perfect to be simple losses. Often, they are deliberately exotic, from Cornwall and Cyprus, Afghanistan and Mycenae. Like the Masai throwing their treasured grass, the more precious an offering, the more its power.

THE POWER OF OFFERINGS

The Thames has disgorged a huge concentration of ancient weapons, including a fine alderwood club from 3000 BC, the 28 Bronze Age swords found by just one Victorian, and the astonishing Celtic Battersea shield from 350 BC. This large, jewel-encrusted bronze masterpiece can be seen in the British Museum, so perfect it looks like a film prop. A museum expert has written a whole book on the shield, and confirms that it was a devotional offering to the river, 'not made for warfare'.

THE ASTONISHING CELTIC BATTERSEA SHIELD FROM 350 BC. THIS LARGE, JEWEL-ENCRUSTED BRONZE MASTERPIECE CAN BE SEEN IN THE BRITISH MUSEUM ... IT WAS A DEVOTIONAL OFFERING TO THE RIVER.

A different Celtic shield, from the Thames at Wandsworth, only reveals a design of birds after you stare at its swirling pattern in a certain way. This was discovered by Barry Cunliffe, Professor of Archaeology at Oxford University, and he says, 'This is the art of shape-shifting'; Celts believed they could easily morph into animals and Cunliffe believes the shield mirrored this. Magical designs were offered to the river of magic.[3]

More morbid things were offered to the river by the severed-head fetishist Celts. The patina on several skulls from Southwark showed that they were put in the river for a little while before being buried.

The Romans had eight temples clustered near the river, including one to Neptune by the river crossing. Their mode of offering weapons to the river was to bend them so completely that they were useless, underlining the sacrifice.

Visiting Vikings also saw sacredness in the Thames, donating a scabbard with a brass wolf's head featuring blue glass eyes (found in 1869, now in the British Museum), and many swords and spears. Munich's Sonia Marzinzik is one of the few people able to decipher water-worn runes. The symbolic runic alphabet was used by Anglo-Saxons, Vikings and Tolkien, who put a message in runes on the cover of *The Hobbit*. (The rune-inscribed Viking ring which inspired him is in the British Museum too.) Marzinzik is convinced that Vikings threw weapons in the river as an act of 'amuletic power', seeking protection from the watery deity.[4] An antiquated practice? No, Panzer commanders had runes on their tanks, 'meaningless scribblings', as Churchill called them.

POWERFUL SYMBOLISM

Words cannot express the feeling behind offering weapons to the Thames, that river of eternity and rebirth. Cunliffe explains that 'chthonic [underworld] deities' live in rivers, and cites a hilarious Marxist theory for the weapon offerings, something about keeping the gold price down, a sort of reverse quantitative easing. The milieu of the offerings is better evoked by works like Mahler's *Resurrection Symphony*, Sibelius's fifth symphony, or AC/DC's *Highway to Hell* – works concerned with eternal recurrence. They evoke the mood of these wandering warrior civilizations better than a pile of books.

The river is both death and life. As with the Ganges, doom and corpses have abounded. Remarkably, the funeral processions of Queen Elizabeth, Henry VII and Lord Nelson were all on the river. Dickens wrote of 'the great black river stretching away to the great ocean Death', and a boatman taunted the artist Bewick nearing the torrents under London Bridge: 'Are ye not *affeared*?'[5]

FISH

But the river has given more life than it has taken, and for most
of its history it has been clean. Fish-killing levels of pollution
reigned for just 140 years, from 1830–1970. Elizabeth I was so
proud of the waters that she conducted international negotiations
on her glass-sided barge. To Spenser it was
the 'silver streaming Thames', and in 1562 a
visiting Venetian thought it 'just as pleasant
as the Grand Canal'. London salmon were
praised for their exquisite taste in 1746.
Blackwall whitebait were another delicacy.

BILLINGSGATE
WAS ITS OWN
WORLD, WITH
'BILLINGSGATE
ENGLISH', A
UNIQUELY FOUL
LANGUAGE

The mystical Thames was respected at
Billingsgate, the riverside fish market so old
that its origin really is 'lost in the mists of time'. King Athelstan
gave it a charter in 940. It may be named after Belin, a Celtic
god who took severed heads to the underworld. Billingsgate
was its own world, with 'Billingsgate English', a uniquely foul
language, pubs allowed to open at 4am (gin and milk a customary
tipple) and, until about 1850, a tradition of offering money on
Midsummer Day at the high altar of the market church.[6] The
porters' leather helmets, which they were still wearing when
I visited in 1968, were derived from the archers' headgear at
Agincourt and were so well made that they were passed down
through generations. The market now covers 5.2 hectares
(13 acres) on a new site in east London.

An enduring fish story tells of a knight who was given a wedding
ring by a wise woman and told he would marry a certain maid.
The maid did not take his fancy so he hurled the ring in the river,
but later on she retrieved the ring when gutting a fish for dinner.
The knight gave in to fate, married her, and was happy. Lady
Berry (died 1696) is persistently associated with the maid, because

of the large ring-in-a-fish carving on her tomb at St Dunstan's Church in Stepney. The tale is evidently part of the world's soul, cropping up in *The Arabian Nights*.

More romantically, Edward Osborne, who dived out of a London Bridge house window in 1536 to rescue an infant girl who had fallen from the window, ended up marrying the girl when she grew up.

FROST FAIRS

The liveliest interludes in river history are the frost fairs, which took place when the river froze, with ice up to 60cm (2ft) thick. The freezes lasted for a surprisingly long time: two months in 1683 and six weeks in 1789, long enough for whole tented streets to emerge.

The festivities were irresistible, with a whole ox often being roasted, presses printing books, skittle alleys, fortune-tellers and fire-eaters. Henry VIII took a sleigh from Whitehall to Greenwich; Elizabeth I went out on the ice and joined an archery competition. In 1688 a coach-and-six thundered from Westminster to London Bridge on the ice.

But the Thames, as always, both gave life and took it. Many fell through the ice. At Rotherhithe, a thawing ice floe broke away and drifted downstream; on it was a frozen-in boat moored to a tavern. The whole tavern was dragged into the freezing waters, killing five sleepers within.

MUSIC

Londoners sang special songs in time to the swirl and surge of this tideway, which the poet Alfred Williams collected just before they were lost, publishing them in 1923. Even everyday calls were songs, as on the steamboats: a boy had to call careful speed directions to the engine-man below, out of sight – 'Stop-aww' (stop), 'Ee-saw' (easy). For centuries before that, water-taxi men cried, like Indian chai-sellers, 'Sculls-sculls-sculls' to advertise their presence.

One freezing day, an old coastal skipper with brass buttons and whiskers called out from a quay to Captain Joseph Conrad, 'Haul away there, haul away!' Conrad, proud of his sailing-ship skills, thought 'Silly old fool', until he saw that his topgallant spars were about to smash a warehouse window.

There was other music on the water. At night, Conrad loved the ships' bells, 'mysterious and muffled in the white vapour from

London Bridge right down to the Nore'. The river promised escape and renewal for Conrad. As an old salt told him, 'Ports are no good. Ships rot and men go to the devil.'[7]

London Bridge Is Falling Down
The song 'London Bridge Is Falling Down' is very old, possibly pre-Conquest, and full of mystery. Who is 'my fair lady'? Many real women have been proposed, none convincingly. After weeks of reading river lore I am convinced she is the river herself.

THE ART OF THE THAMES

Conrad the Polish sailor caught some of the river's essence, its Dickensian potential for resurrection and for apocalypse. His *Heart of Darkness* starts placidly on it and ends with horrors. An American in late Victorian London, James Whistler, also spent decades circling its essence. He looked out on it from his upstairs rooms at 7 Lindsey Row, Chelsea, and sketched and painted it endlessly, often from small boats in midstream. Recognizable at first, the pictures became increasingly impressionistic, until he evoked the waterway with just a few blue bars, or a sparkly wash of paint. These pictures are now his most admired, but the critic Ruskin attacked them so virulently that Whistler brought a libel case against him.

And so it came to pass that the full might of the English legal system examined the essence of the Thames. It was 1878. At the

Old Bailey a picture was exhibited in court, upside down, and Whistler was grilled by a barrister: 'Do you say this is a correct representation?'

Later in the trial, an exasperated attorney general barked at Whistler, 'Do you really expect 200 guineas for two days' work?' 'No,' he replied, 'for the knowledge of a lifetime.' Court Number

AN EXASPERATED ATTORNEY GENERAL BARKED AT WHISTLER, 'DO YOU REALLY EXPECT 200 GUINEAS FOR TWO DAYS' WORK?' 'NO,' HE REPLIED, 'FOR THE KNOWLEDGE OF A LIFETIME.' COURT NUMBER ONE BURST INTO APPLAUSE.

One burst into applause. The artist won, but was awarded a farthing and bankrupted by the case. Further saddened by the building of the Embankment along his beloved river, he went to live in Venice.

He would have got on with Rotherhithe-born Douglas Chellow, whom the journalist Charles Whitehead met in 1878; 'He wrung his hands as if finding all hopeless, and then suddenly quietened and was all smiles. It seemed he only wanted to convey his love of the Thames', which he saw as an 'ancient deity'. He lived in a shack on the riverbank at Greenwich, where he daily 'made obeisance to the river'.[9]

The same spirit animated the Arts and Crafts printer Thomas Cobden-Sanderson. A hawk-faced idealist who always wore a sky-blue smock, he ran the Doves Press before the First World War, near the Dove pub at Hammersmith. His books were painstakingly handmade and he threw used brass type off Hammersmith Bridge at night, 'giving his work back to the river of life'. The river itself seems to have got the general idea: it swept the urn with his ashes out of the niche in his garden wall and bore it downriver.

RITUALS

Another of the river's ritual connections was discovered in 1928 by an obscure writer called A. J. Linney. He observed several East Enders at Syon, opposite Brentford, gathering willow twigs on the riverbank. One old man, who had been doing this since late Victorian times, explained that they sold the twigs to Jews in the East End for use during Sukkot, their harvest festival.[10]

Indians are reconsecrating the river. In 2004, a Hindu shrine was found on the bank near Battersea, and both Hindus and Sikhs are campaigning for permission to scatter the ashes of their dead on the Thames.

HEART AND SOUL OF LONDON

Wildlife is returning fast, to re-enchant the river. Terns, sand martins and water voles – like Ratty in *The Wind in the Willows* – are again easy to spot.

Parks are the lungs of London and the river is its soul. Ever since the first Neolithic band of hunters came upon the untamed Thames, marsh-fringed and rippled by beavers, mankind has been able to agree with the French philosopher Gaston Bachelard: 'I cannot sit down by a river without falling into a profound reverie, without looking back over my happiness.'

Notes

1. O. Gurney, *The Hittites* (Pelican, 1952), p.192. Sir James Frazer, *Folklore in the Old Testament* (Macmillan, 1923), pp.252–58 and *The Golden Bough: A Study in Magic and Religion* (Macmillan, 1922), pp.126–27.

2. Cathy Ross and John Clark, *London: The Illustrated History* (Museum of London/ Allen Lane, 2008), p.21.

3. Barry Cunliffe, *The Celts* (Oxford University Press, 2003), pp.68–69.

4. S. Marzinzik, *Masterpieces: Early Medieval Art* (British Museum Press, 2012), p.135.

5 Charles Dickens, *Our Mutual Friend* (1864); Jenny Uglow, *Nature's Engraver: A Life of Thomas Bewick* (Faber, 2006), p.98.

6. John Timbs, *Curiosities of London* (Hotten, 1867), p.185.

7. Joseph Conrad, *The Mirror of the Sea* (Doubleday, 1924), p.128.

8. Margaret MacDonald's *An American in London: Whistler and the Thames* (Dulwich Picture Gallery, 2013) has amazing pictures, gathered together for the first time.

9. Peter Ackroyd, *Thames: Sacred River* (Chatto and Windus, 2007), p.184. This great barque of a book stands out from all the bumboats of Thames literature.

10. A. G. Linney, *The Peepshow of the Port of London* (Sampson Low, 1929), p.232.

INDEX